# GAIL DEVERS

# MY LIFE IN

# STORY:

# STRONGER

# GAIL DEVERS

# MY LIFE IN

# STORY:

# STRONGER

**By Gail Devers and Braxton A. Cosby**

Cosby Media Productions™

Entertaining the Mind, and Inspiring the Soul

Published by Cosby Media Productions.
www.cosbymediaproductions.com
Cover art: Cosby Media Productions
Edited by: Tamar Hela
**ISBN 10: 1537713329**
**ISBN 13: 978-1537713328**

# TABLE OF CONTENTS

# ACKNOWLEDGEMENTS

In writing this book, I do realize it wasn't done alone. The contributions of many produced this project and must be acknowledged.

Chelan, you worked tirelessly with Leon from Cosby Media Productions, who set the wheels in motion.

The team at CMP: You believed in the vision and took a chance. I must say it was both liberating and exciting. I relived experiences, remembering emotions in order to get it on paper.

Braxton, you are a joy to work with. You made the process easy, quick, and painless. Thanks for the countless hours of collaborating and listening; your innovative and creative mind is one I treasure.

Kenny Mitchell, you are a master whiz in graphic design. Mike, you said "yes, it needs to be told" and took on extra duties—taking pictures for the book, your photography is stunning. You love and support me as always. You and the girls gave me time to devote to this, when you would have preferred that I be the one playing dolls.

Karsen and Legacy: I love your ideas, frankness, and ever-honest opinions. Your view of Mommy stepping from the track in spikes to the next part of my life in high heels with "a little bling" was just what the book cover needed.

Those who have gone before me: your contributions are immeasurable.

"Lil Big Momma:" you gave me your strength, tenacity, and the age of 100 to shoot for.

Dad, "my biggest fan:" the Pac Man games were the best, and you gave me your family to love and your son, Mike who walks in your footprints.

Mima and Papa: you gave me my DNA—just the right mixture of you both to make me who I am, with eternal love and support.

Kenneth and Parenthesis you "pushed" me into my career and prepared me for life, as big brothers should.

Way too many to name, but every track, weight training and rehab facility, all my friends, past relationships and acquaintances... you helped me to hone my craft, grow, and learn.

Debra Anderson, I finally put my thoughts to

print: "Dream Realized."

And utmost thanks, love, and honor to God for creating me. Thanks for placing stumbling blocks and bright lights on my path, and seeing me to and through them all. You gave me experiences and adventures which resulted in the ultimate gift. A life that can now be told in stories.

# PART I: STARTING BLOCKS

# CHAPTER 1

"Miss Devers!" a voice calls out to me from behind.

I turn to find an older-looking, petite, red-haired woman racing towards me in a bright-colored set of high-heeled shoes. "Yes?" I ask.

She stops just short of stepping on my shoes, and pauses to catch her breath, panting. "I tried to catch you back there in the office while you were signing in, but I was delayed in the hallway by a parent." She offers her hand to me. "I'm Mrs. Stephens, the Assistant Principal. Welcome to Tyler Ponds Elementary."

I reach for her hand. "Oh, wonderful. Thank you for having me."

She squeezes and flashes a warm smile. "No, thank *you* for coming. Especially on such short notice. I was afraid that we'd have a gaping hole in our Awards Outreach Program."

"Chelan caught up with me just in time. I was about to book another event out of town, but everything stops when it comes to the kids."

"Thankfully." She gestures me back down the hall, in the direction from which she came. "I don't know if anyone in the office had a chance to brief you, but you'll be speaking to the third graders today for the most part, split into two groups, over the span of one hour. Should expect about thirty or forty kids."

"No problem."

"They ask a lot of questions, so I hope you brought something to drink? If not, I can get you something."

I hold up a bottle of water. "I'm good."

"Excellent. You'll be speaking in the library. It's our biggest room in the building. Coming off a fresh renovation last year. You'll love it. With all the kids inside, it will be quite the cozy little spot."

"Okie dokie," I reply.

We get to the entrance of the library, and no sooner do we enter than I'm greeted by a row of the brightest teeth I've ever seen, attached to an even wider smile. "Gail Devers, so glad to finally meet you in person. My name is Daryl Lenchcomb. I'm the school librarian. Huge fan of yours."

His hand swallows mine in an instant, complete with matching calluses on each palm. Aah, a man not afraid of a good days work. Just like my dad. "Hello," I reply.

"I used to run the hurdles in college at Old Alabama State." He hops in place a few times, cycling his right leg. The sight breaks a smile across my face. "Never could get that trail leg to snap down as quickly as I'd liked to. Nowhere near as fast as yours. If it wasn't for that last hurdle in the—"

"Mr. Lenchcomb, if you are done," starts Mrs. Stephens, with a glare, "we'd like to get Miss Devers over to the area where the children will be setting up."

Lenchcomb snaps in place like a sharp puzzle. "Yes, ma'am," he says, offering a salute as he escorts us to the back portion of the library.

It's like Mrs. Stephens has said: the room is beautifully renovated with plush carpet, countless aisles of books, brand new computers, and comfy-looking chairs. We take a seat at a long, mahogany wooden table, and I take a swig of my water.

"Miss Devers, this is where we will sit once the children come in," says Mrs. Stephens. She looks to her watch momentarily. "They should be here in about five

3

minutes or so. Once they are settled, I will introduce you and say a few words about your accomplishments. Anything in particular you'd like me to say?"

I shake my head. "Nah, that won't be necessary. I speak from the heart."

"Great."

Just as Mrs. Stephens leans in to speak once more, a low rumbling of feet interrupts her, growing louder and louder by the second. She turns her attention to the far corner of the room, where an army of third graders marches in our direction.

She waves them over, with her index finger firmly pressed against her lips. "This way," she whispers.

The kids file inside, taking a seat in front of us, shoulder to shoulder in rows of fifteen to twenty. I offer a few friendly waves as they stare back at me. One child, a little girl with the tightest set of pig-tails I've ever seen, gets out a: "You're so pretty," before anyone can stop her.

I mouth: "So are you," in my lowest voice.

After several minutes of commotion, everyone appears set, and Mrs. Stephens takes her place out front. "Children of Tyler Ponds Elementary School, you are in for a special treat. In keeping with the celebration of today's recipients of the Awards Outreach Program, we have a very special guest speaker here today. Many of you probably don't know her, but know *of* her. She is a multi-award-winning Olympic Gold medalist and World Champion sprinter in both—" she turns to wave at me. "Help me out if I mess up, Gail. In the hurdles, one hundred meter sprint, and the four by one hundred meter relay. Right?"

I nod. "Exactly."

"She has a marvelous story to share with you all about her life, the challenges she faced, and the hardships she overcame to achieve her goals. We always preach perseverance to you, and Gail is a shining example of how hard work pays off. Without any further ado, please give a warm welcome to Mrs. Gail Devers."

The library erupts in a wave of handclaps that seems to shake the books free from their shelves. I stand and join Mrs. Stephens. "Thank you, everyone. I am so glad to be here today." Mrs. Stephens leaves to take her seat behind me. "Now, before I begin, I'd like to see, by a show of hands, who actually knows who I am?"

One solitary hand rises to the ceiling, attached to a small boy with the cutest little chubby cheeks sitting in the front row. Before I can ask him a question, the girl next to him swats it down. "Stop lying, Billy," she says. She looks over to me with a cute set of puppy eyes. "Sorry, Miss Devers."

I wave her off. "It's perfectly fine. You all don't know me, and I don't know you, so I consider us all even. That way, I don't have to try to impress you, and everyone here can feel comfortable asking me questions. I just have one rule: please raise your hand before you speak, so that everyone can get a turn. Does that sound like a plan?"

A chorus of, "Yes," rings out before me.

"Great. So, let me see...where will I start first?"

"How about: where you were born?" a young girl blurts out.

"Tamika Johnson, didn't Miss Devers just say to raise your hand first?" asks Mrs. Stephens.

"But, no one else was talking, so I thought it was a good idea, Mrs. Stephens. Sorry," Tamika says.

"That's fine," I reply with a wink. "Good question to start with."

# CHAPTER 2

"Alave, please. The doctor said he will be here soon," the nurse said.

"Larry, get this woman out of my face," Alave lashed out, her hand just below the rim of her belly.

Larry stepped forward, and escorted the nurse over to the doorway of the room. "Look: my wife is convinced that this is going to happen sometime today, and she is not going to take no for an answer." He paused, searching the nurse's eyes for justification. "You have to understand my place. I will not be able to sleep if I take her back home. Do you want that on your conscience?"

The nurse eyed Alave, who sat at the edge of the evaluation table, speeding through a series of breathing exercises. "She's not even dilated yet, and the examination showed the baby hasn't completely turned around." She sighed. "I guess there's no way of getting out of this one."

He smiled. "Exactly."

The nurse was paged and turned to the door. "I've got another call coming in from a high risk patient down the hallway. I will have someone check for vacancies, and will come and get your things as soon as a room is confirmed."

"Thank you," Larry said. He returned to his wife and held her hand. "It's going to be all right, darling. Just hold on a little while longer."

"I'm not playing around, Larry. I know this baby is coming tonight. I don't care what that doctor says. How many babies has he had?"

"Need I remind you that the doctor you're referring to is the same one that delivered Parenthesis?"

"I know. But I don't care." Alave flashed a smile, and returned to her breathing.

Moments later, two orderlies came to the door, along with a wheelchair and a fresh gown. "Someone here to take a ride?" the taller one asked.

"Yes!" Alave screamed, sliding off the edge of the table.

"Easy," said Larry. "Don't let this baby slip out in the emergency room."

Alave walked over to the wheelchair and took a seat. They whisked her off to the fifth floor, where her room was waiting for her. Larry helped her to the bed, and placed her belongings in the closet. He took a seat next to her, and gently rubbed the back of her hand. "Remember when Parenthesis came?"

"Yep. The sun was just as bright as it is today."

"You mean, the one hiding behind the clouds?"

Alave shook her head, smiling. "Yes. What do you expect, Larry? It *is* Seattle, for heaven's sake."

A knock at the door caught their attention. "Hello, folks. My name is Nurse Nancy, and I will be taking care of you this shift." She began writing her name on the chalkboard next to the bathroom. "This is my number if you need me."

Alave leaned forward in the bed, looking past Larry. "Any idea where my –" She paused, and glanced over to Larry. "I mean...my *doctor* is, Nancy?"

Nancy smiled. "It's okay. You don't have to hold your tongue ma'am. Most doctors are called much worse on this wing. He phoned in the minute we assigned you a room. He's convinced that you won't be having this baby 'til Monday. So you can rest easy."

Alave slumped back into the pillow and sighed heavily.

"Nancy, is there any way we can get her something to drink?" asked Larry.

"Certainly. Feel free to slip into that gown as well. These rooms have a tendency to get kind of hot. I'll come back later to examine you."

"Thank you," said Alave.

After a few hours, Larry dozed off in the recliner, while Alave fought like mad to get into a comfortable position. She turned a few times until finally, the urge to use the bathroom came upon her like a raging sea. She slipped to the side of the bed as quiet as she could, so as not to wake up Larry. Slipping on her shoes, she began walking towards the bathroom.

Suddenly, she felt a warm sensation run down the inside of her legs. She froze and squeezed her knees together. "Larry!" she screamed.

Larry catapulted from his chair with a loud, "What is it?"

The color drained from his face as he spotted Alave, halfway between the bed and the bathroom, standing in a pool of fluid, one hand on her stomach and the other between her legs, knees clenched together.

"I need help; she's coming," Alave said.

Larry screamed for help. A pair of nurses rushed into the room and helped Larry lift Alave to the bed. An hour later, the screams of a baby interrupted the calm of the hallway.

Larry rocked the baby in his arms and leaned her down so that Alave could lay eyes on her. "Isn't she beautiful, baby?"

"Gorgeous. And look at those eyes," said Alave.

"Yep. She's already looking around. Doctor said she came out feet first, kicking. I think she's going to be a runner," Larry said.

"Oh, Larry, that don't mean nothing."

Larry stood up, gently bouncing the baby in his arms. "What should we name her?"

Alave turned to the window, admiring the stormy wind and rain. "Well, she was born in a storm. Let's call her Gail."

# CHAPTER 3

"And that's how I was born," I say.

"Wow, you came out feet first? That's so cool!" says a little boy next to Tamika.

"My mommy said that's called a beached birth," Tamika says.

I smile, on the verge of hysteria. "No, baby, it's called a breeched birth."

"That's enough, Tamika. You may sit down now. Let someone else take a turn at asking questions," says Mrs. Stephens.

I scan the pack of children, my eyes finally resting on a boy in the back row. I point at him. "You, with the blue sweater. Do you have a question?"

"Please, stand up, Robert, and tell everyone your name," says Mrs. Stephens.

"My name is Robert Davis, and I wanted to know if you walked early since you came out landing on your feet."

My cheeks flush. "Very good question, Robert. Actually, it must've meant something, because I learned how to walk at seven months, and I was potty trained at nine months."

"Good heavens!" blurted Mrs. Stephens.

"Yep. Made life around the house real interesting, real early."

"When did you learn to run?" asks Tamika.

"Again, Tamika?" asks Mrs. Stephens, sounding exasperated.

"I remember being only six at the time. My brother, Parenthesis, and my god-brother, Kenneth, used to always go to Kenneth's house around the corner. And because I was the smallest, they made me walk since we only had two bikes. One day, I decided to take a shortcut, and beat them there. Well, after cutting through a dark alley, they found me on the street with about half a city block left to get to Kenneth's house.

So, I started on a mad dash. I could feel the wind blowing through me, and passing over my ears, making a loud noise as if it was screaming at me. Kenneth and my brother didn't make anything easy for me, so they tried their hardest to catch me. But it was too late. I crashed in the front yard of Kenneth's house, just seconds before they got there. To this day, Parenthesis brags that he and

Kenneth are the reason I started running, and that they take full credit for being my first coaches."

A hand raises, and I see it from the corner of my vision. "Stand up, and tell everyone your name, dear."

"My name is Kendra Taylor, and I wanted to know if you ever got beat up by your older brother?"

"Did I..." I say wryly.

# CHAPTER 4

"Ow!" I screamed as Parenthesis added another pillow to my head while I curled up into a tighter ball in the corner of my room.

I could hear the rumble of my mother's feet grow louder as Parenthesis carried on. A loud slapping noise stopped the beating.

"What are you doing, boy? Leave your sister alone," Mima commanded.

I finally un-raveled from my protective ball, and opened my eyes.

"I was just playing," Parenthesis said.

Mima grabbed him by the arm firmly, pinching a good inch of his skin between her fingers and thumb. "I told you to clean your room. Get in there, and do what I said."

Parenthesis screamed and pulled away, rubbing the reddened area with his hand. He turned to me and grinned before leaving. I pulled to the side of the bed, and Mima sat down next to me. "You all right, baby?"

I nodded. "Yeah. He can't *really* hurt me, Mima."

She wrapped her arm around my shoulders and pulled me close. "I know. But you know, Gail, until you get even with him, he won't stop trying."

"What am I to do? I'm only seven years old, and he's both older and bigger than me."

"Everyone has a spot of vulnerability, baby. All you have to do is find his. You don't need to necessarily hurt him, but just make him *really* uncomfortable. Once you expose him, he'll learn to leave you alone."

"How do you know for sure?"

She smiled. "I know a thing or two about bullies."

This made me sit up. "Really?"

"Yeah, really."

"Oh, Mima, please tell me," I pleaded.

"Well," she started, "I once knew a girl named Sonya. She terrorized everybody on the block: kicking and punching people like crazy, any chance she got. Her father was a local boxer and taught her everything she knew. So, she liked to take it out on all the other kids. I used to ride the bus with her, and it made me an easy target. I would intentionally sit in the front of the bus most days, and get off as soon as I could, and start running home before she could catch me. But one day, there were no empty seats, and I had to sit behind her."

My eyes widened. "Mima, what did you do?"

"Well, I was terrified, to say the least. I kept thinking all the way home: *How am I going to get myself out of this*? At the last stop sign before we got home, the idea came to me. In the yard across the street, I saw a dog chasing his tail." She laughed. "He was just turning in circles, over and over again. And that was the secret. No matter how hard he tried, he'd never catch it because it'd always be one step ahead of him. I had to stay one step ahead of Sonya."

"But how, Mima?"

"I was smaller – much like you are smaller than your brother – but that made me quicker. So when I got off the bus, Sonya was standing there waiting for me. I jumped off the bus and ran behind her. She turned to find me, but every time she turned, I turned with her. Over and over again she tried to catch me, but I avoided her each time. Soon, a group of kids began to gather around and laugh at Sonya. She started to scream at the top of her lungs. One by one, the other kids laughed all the more, pointing and carrying on like they were at the circus. Sonya got bright red and finally gave up, running all the way home. After that, she refused to even look at me. Kids knew where she was vulnerable, so she left them alone as well."

"That's amazing, Mima. But I don't think that's going to work on Parenthesis. He's faster than me."

Mima leaned in, and kissed me on the head. "Maybe there's something else, baby. Perhaps, you should try looking at his feet," she said in a whisper.

His feet.

She was right. Parenthesis had very sensitive feet. He always wore socks around the house because he couldn't stand the feeling of the cold, rough floor. All it'd take was one good attack on those crooked toes of his, and maybe, just maybe, he'd leave me alone.

That night, I made my plan to hit him where it hurt. After dinner, Parenthesis loved to recline on the couch and take a nap. That's when I'd strike.

I waited a while until Mima and Papa cleared from the kitchen, and peered into the living room, waiting for Parenthesis to take his position. Like clockwork, there he was, passed out, toes kicked atop the coffee table. I tiptoed over to the table, pulled his socks off slowly, and bent his toes back as far as my little hands could stretch them.

Parenthesis awoke with a low, "Ow!" that shook the house.

Mima and Papa came running, and I cleared over to the edge of the couch where Parenthesis could not get to me. Papa squatted down next to Parenthesis. "What is it, boy? Tell me what happened."

Beneath a stream of tears, my older brother found the strength to murmur, "Gail did it. She pulled my toes back."

Mima and Papa looked over to me, the blood halfway drained from Mima's face. "Did you do that, Gail? Is it true?" Papa asked.

I stayed silent, only giving a faint nod. Mima looked over to Papa as her hand rose to cover her mouth. Papa did the same as he patted Parenthesis on the back. "There, there, boy. I don't think they're broken. You'll be fine. Come and put some ice on it."

He lifted Parenthesis from the couch and walked him to the kitchen. Mima knelt down before me, her hands caressing my shoulders. "Nice job, baby," she said with a wink.

## CHAPTER 5

"I bet he never tried to beat you up again, huh?" asks Kendra.

"Err...sometimes. But not as much, for sure," I say.

"It sounds like your brother had it coming. Just like mine does, Miss Devers," says Kendra, pounding her fist into her hand.

"No, I'd never advocate violence, baby. But, it is important to stand up for yourself, and to know how to best your opponent. It's not always about strength or speed. Sometimes, you have to use your head. It's a lesson that served me well in competition."

Another hand rises directly in front of me. A young boy stands and smiles proudly, despite his missing two front teeth.

"Jimmy, say your full name please," says Mrs. Stephens.

He clears his throat. "My name is Jimmy Lawrence. I wanted to know if other kids in the neighborhood ever teased you. If so, what did you do about it?"

"Well Jimmy, my family was known as the *hood* version of the *Beavers.*"

His eyebrows bunch and his mouth cocks to the side. "Who's that?"

"Oh, I'm showing my age. You don't know who the Beavers are because they were way before your time." He still considers me with a bewildered gaze. I wave him off. "Don't worry about it. Just think of my family as a very pleasant, fun-loving one that never got into any kind of trouble and did their best to keep the peace in the neighborhood. That being said, no one really messed with me, or my brother—*especially* my brother, because he knew all the head dudes on the street anyway. So, I got a free pass. People were always wary not to bother Parenthesis' little sister."

The bell rings, and the kids begin to disperse. Mrs. Stephens looks down at her watch. "Oh, my, where did the time go?" She walks into the cloud of kids, waving her hands frantically. "Quickly, grab your things and follow your teacher back to your rooms. We have another group coming in."

With the departure of the first group, another flood of even more tiny souls comes, each one sporting a curious guise upon their faces as they enter.

I take my seat at the table and sip on my water. One girl breaks from the pack, and steps up to me. "I heard that you are a fast runner. I bet you can't beat my brother. He's in the sixth grade."

"Really? And what grade do you think I'm in?"

"You're too old to still be in school. So, I know you're too old to still be fast. He could probably beat you with his eyes closed."

I bite down on my bottom lip to stifle my smile. "You're probably right. What's your name?"

"My name is Dawntrel Willis. My momma name is Dawn and my daddy name is Trelvin."

"That's quite an original name, Dawntrel."

"Dawntrel, please take a seat on the floor," says Mrs. Stephens, closing in from behind.

As the troop of about twenty–five or so kids file in to the library, Mrs. Stephens does her best to align them on the floor; shoulder to shoulder, feet crisscrossed out in front. She introduces me again, and I stand to give a wave. Just as I'm about to speak, I hear Dawntrel mumbling.

"What is it, Dawntrel? Would you like to share with the class?" I ask. I shoot a quick glance over to Mrs. Stephens, and then back to Dawntrel.

"I was just saying maybe my brother couldn't beat you running after all," Dawntrel says.

"What made you change your mind?"

She looks me up and down, before finally resting on my legs. She points just below my knees. "Them big-ole legs you got. You could probably crush soda cans with those."

"Um, that's enough, Dawntrel," interrupts Mrs. Stephens. "Where are your manners?"

"It's fine, Mrs. Stephens," I assure her. "I'm used to it. I get that a lot. You make a great point, Dawntrel. Actually, I'll share a little story with you about my big-ole legs."

# CHAPTER 6

"You going out for the track team this year, Gail?" Sandy asked.

We passed a set of lockers on our way upstairs, and I only answer with a shoulder shrug. It wasn't until we finally came to a stop in front of Miss Snow's fifth period English class that I answered. "I'm not sure."

"Why not? You're like the fastest girl in the school."

"I know. It's just...I hate running. And I don't like the way people stare at my legs."

"Please tell me you're kidding? I'd kill for a set of legs like that. Look at these tree stumps. Better than having a set of *kankles*."

I shook my head. "Besides, nobody is going to root for *Sweet Polly Purebred* anyway."

"You still worried about that stupid name they gave you? Gail, you have a good heart, and you always do the right thing. So what? Shouldn't you? Ever since I met you when you moved out here to San Diego, I've known you to do exactly what you want to do. Stubborn as a mule." She nudged me as we walked in the classroom. "Don't change now just because we are in the tenth grade."

"But what about all my other friends? You know they'll hate me if I start beating them."

"You made the choice to stay at Sweetwater, and they decided to go to Douglas Turner High School. You can't be penalized for that."

"I know. I just miss them sometimes. Don't you?"

"I could, but my mom and dad didn't give me choice. They said Sweetwater was better. And when your father is the principal, well... it ain't like I had a choice."

My eyebrow rose. "True."

"Kick their butts. I'll be rooting for you. My mother always says that if you don't use the gifts God gives you, you'll lose them. Why waste all that talent? Do something with it."

Sandy's words clung to my brain like warm honey.

*Use your gifts. How could I think any differently?*

My grandmother said something like that years ago, referencing some story from the Bible about talents. Jesus told the people to be mindful about wasting what God gave us. I made up my mind.

*I had to run.*

And run, I did.

Tryouts were a breeze. Most girls could barely take the West Coast heat, much less handle an hour-long practice session. But me, I endured both with ease. We lived for the summer, me and my brother. We stayed outside all day until the street lights came on and Mima and Papa came looking for us. So, the sun was never an issue. Plus, running against my brother and the neighborhood boys all the time made me both quick and strong. I could run for hours before needing to stop.

One afternoon, just as I was finishing up one of the longest, most grueling practice sessions I ever had, Coach Alim made the decision that changed my track career for life.

"Gail," Coach Alim started, looking at his stopwatch. "That was a mighty fine time you posted in the four hundred earlier. Ever thought of running the sprints?" His thick mustache wrinkled as he stared at me.

"No, sir. I've always trained for middle distance, ever since practicing with my brother over the summers and into cross country. It's all I've known."

"I know your history, running at the state meet last year in both the eight and the four was impressive, stealing two San Diego county records in the process. But I really think you're missing a calling here. You got power, quickness, and obviously a whole boatload of stamina. I think that if you lower the distance down a bit, you'd cream the rest of the competition. You could even win a state title someday."

I could feel my heart racing as he spoke, along with my eyebrows bunching together. The idea seemed sound, but I had never truly considered the option before. I was comfortable with where I was. I was doing exactly what Sandy suggested: using my gifts. Any lofty goals of beating people and wining state title – although it had its merit – were far from my mind.  Still, the competitor inside me, the one my brother helped to create from all those trials and tests growing up, hungered to see if I could actually do it.

"Sure," I said with a shrug.

"Great. We'll start you on the three hundred hurdles. It's a step down from the four hundred, and all you have to do it jump over eight hurdles along the way."

"Okie dokie. Sounds easy enough."

"Okay." Coach Alim twirled his stopwatch around his fingers one time, and slipped it into his pants pocket. "I'll set up a lane tomorrow and let you give it a whirl." He began to walk off.

"Um, Coach?" I called out. He turned to find my gaze. "How will I know if I'm a hurdler? What if I fall down?"

"If you fall down, that doesn't mean anything. But if you get back up and still want to try again, well," he paused with a smile, "then we'll know something for sure."

I nodded. Running home that night, I kept the event switch a secret, afraid that Parenthesis would over-scrutinize me and scare off the prospect of trying something new.

The next day at practice, things ran just as before. I ran my two warm-up laps. The team went through all the drills and stretches together. Then things changed.

"Gail and Phedra, you two come over here with me. The rest of you will go with Coach Ceja," said Coach Alim.

We followed Coach Alim to the other side of the track, where one lane was filled with six hurdles, running half the length of the straight away, with the rest bending into the curve. To my surprise, Coach Alim bypassed the hurdles and headed over to the fence.

"Come with me, girls." He turned sideways and laid one hand on the fence, with the other on his hip. "Now, this is our first drill. To be a hurdler, you have to be flexible." He began to swing the leg closest to the fence forward and back, resembling a swing at the playground. "What you need to do is swing your leg, like this, ten times. And then, turn around, face the other way, and do the other leg. Three sets."

I jumped right in, grabbing the fence with my right hand and swinging the same leg forward and back. After a count of ten, I flipped around and did the left side. "Like that, Coach?"

Coach Alim stroked his beard for a moment, and then stepped closer. "Gail, I want you to fold your fingers together, kinda like a chain."

I did what he asked without question.

"I thought so. You're a righty."

"A *righty*? What's that mean?"

"You lead with your right leg. That's the leg that will cross the hurdle first."

I shook my head. "But how did you know?"

"Well, I saw which one you kicked the highest on that fence drill, then when I asked you to weave your fingers together, your right one came out on top. It was consistent with what I've seen from hurdlers before. Old coaching trick. Never fails." He stopped to wave at Phedra. "Phedra, come over here."

Phedra turned out to be a lefty; something Coach Alim seemed to celebrate.

"I like it when I have two different leads; gives me something to compare with drills and such." He took his cap off and scratched at his head, as if trying to free up a thought. "Okay, girls. The next drill is going to teach you how to use your trail leg. Scratch that. Let's just get into it. We can clean things up later." He headed back to the track. "Gail, you're up first."

I stepped back on to the track, and followed him to the lane with the hurdles.

"What I want you to do is skip forward and then as you get closer to the hurdles, take a stab at jumping over it, with your right leg first. Make any adjustments you need to as you get closer to the hurdle, but don't make it too late. You'll fall flat on your face. Got it?" he said.

He drifted off into the inside of the asphalt oval, and watched from the grass. I got in a halfway three-point stance and focused on the hurdle. I looked over at him. "Right leg first, right?"

This time, Coach Alim only answered with a head nod. The silence sent a chill all over my body. It was like he was detaching himself from anything that had to do with my demise. I was alone.

Just me and that first hurdle.

I ran at mid-speed and approached the first one. With about five meters left, I made a quick step, followed by a long one, driving my left foot into the ground and lifting my right one skyward. Before I knew it, I had cleared the hurdle and landed safely on the other side.

My heart leapt into my throat. "Coach!" I screamed over the choking feeling. "I did it!"

"Yes, you did, Gail." He pointed down the track. "Now, clear the other seven."

"What?"

"You heard me; finish." He clapped his hands. "We're burning daylight here."

I took off, using the last bit of fleeting adrenaline in my veins to clear the next seven, with even less effort than the first. When I finished, Coach Alim found me on the other side of the track.

"Not bad at all, Gail. I timed your landing and take-offs while you were doing it. I haven't seen anything like this before."

"That bad, huh?"

His eyebrows rose. "Are you kidding me? This is not a fluke. You were meant to do this."

"Really?"

"Yes. Are you prepared to win the state?"

"Okie dokie, Coach. If you say so."

He pulled his cap down snugly on his head and turned away. "Again," he said over his shoulder. Then he yelled over to Phedra. "Come on, you're next!"

We must've run those hurdle drills over a dozen times before I actually felt tired. By the time we finished, both Phedra and I had learned to snap down our trail legs, and even lean forward a little while doing so.

"That's a wrap, girls. Great job, both of you. See you tomorrow for the next drill."

I went home that night, overjoyed. It was the first time since running that I actually liked it a little. Not because I thought I was the next great hurdler, but because I had learned something new. Track and field was finally exciting, and regardless of how well I did, I prayed the feeling would stick with me eternally. I decided to keep the day's events from my family, at least until I decided if doing the hurdles were really for me or not.

# CHAPTER 7

"Did you ever fall, Miss Devers?" asks Dawntrel.

"All the time." I lift up my left pants leg just enough to reveal my knee cap. "See that scar right there? My first bad fall, ever. It's stuck with me to this day."

"Yeah, I guess you'd beat my brother running then," Dawntrel says with a smile.

"Maybe," I confess.

"Another question, back there on the end. Avery, is that you?" asks Mrs. Stephens.

A boy – seemingly larger than the other kids his age – stands to his feet and pulls his shirt down over his belly. "Yes. I wanted to know if you missed running the middle-distance races?"

"Good question, Avery. The short answer to that is no. But the long answer comes from my not-so-successful first stab at running the shorter races. Well, remember I said that I kept the truth about switching races from my family? That didn't last very long, because it seems as though Coach Alim was a little overzealous and spilled the beans to a friend of his who was a really good buddy of my Papa's.

"Apparently, he had phoned my father and told him about the change, saying that Coach Alim had never seen anything like it before. So, when I got home, my family already knew, but was testing me to see how long before I'd 'fess up. After about a week, they cornered me, and made me spill the beans over dinner."

"So, what's the long story about then?" asks Avery.

"Oh, yeah. About that," I say.

## CHAPTER 8

"Today's the big day, Gail and Phedra. It's a small meet, but it will give you a chance to run over a full flight of hurdles against some competition other than yourselves."

"Can't wait, Coach. This should be fun," I said.

His eyes panned from Phedra to me. "You sick, Devers?"

"No, why?" I replied.

"Most people aren't this excited about tackling the hurdle for the first time." Coach Alim eyed Phedra curiously. "Look at Phedra; she's shaking like a leaf."

"I guess I just figure I have nothing to lose. At least I'm doing something different."

"I'll be fine, Coach, as soon as I get warmed up," said Phedra.

"All right, well. You girls stay up here in the stands until I call for you. Then I want you to go through all the drills, just like I showed you around the south side of the track. I'll be down there to take you through a few other ones as we get closer to the race. This meet is based only on time, no finals. So run the fastest you can. Got it?"

"Yes, Coach," we said in unison.

The meet got going in the usual fashion, with the one hundred meter hurdles first, followed by the one hundred meter sprint. I took little interest to it at the time, because my new race had only to do with running a good portion of the track while trying to survive over hurdles; although, Coach Alim *did* hint at trying me out in the shorter one at a later time.

The meet sped by in what seemed like thirty minutes, and before too long, Coach Alim was waving us down for warm-ups.

Phedra was the more well-equipped one of us for the hurdles. She towered over me by at least a foot, and her long legs made it easy for her to virtually step over the barriers with ease. I, on the other hand, had to exert some effort to clear the hurdles, due to my stocky build.

Maybe it was my thick calves that kept me short? Who knew?

Regardless of *why*, I decided to focus on the inevitable. It was time to run.

Phedra was up first, pulling the draw for the inside lane. *Lucky*. I could only pray I'd pull that one as well. I dreaded the outside. Not being able to see anyone for the entire race would be a nightmare for me.

When the gun went off, Phedra tore out of the blocks, and made up the stagger on lane two before she crossed the first hurdle. She was really doing well. My eyes fixed on her as she cleared the second and third, until the starter called my name. "Devers, pull your bullet."

He held out his hand, and placed several bullets in a cup, offering it to me. I reached inside blindly and pulled out one. The number eight stabbed at my eyes. The butterflies in my stomach awakened.

The dreaded outside lane.

I handed it back to him and made my way over to my lane. Setting up my blocks was another story. Being a middle distance runner last year, this was new to me. Never did I have to factor coming up from the track or timing the gun. By the time I set my blocks and stripped off my sweat pants, Phedra crossed the finish line in seconds.

Strategically, I wore longer than normal socks – the kind you'd see basketball players wear – in hopes to hide my over-sized calves. It was a mixed bag in determining if that worked or not. Some people ignored me while others, mainly guys, gawked.

It was the voice of the starter that brought me back to reality. *Can't think about socks now. Nor boys, or girls. Only one thing: the sound of the starting pistol.*

"On your marks," the starter announced.

I loaded into my blocks, left leg first, followed by my right. My elbows locked and my shoulder froze.

"Get set," he continued.

My hips rose.

Boom!

The gun went off, and the last thing I remembered was seeing my left foot fly up into my periphery. I drove as hard as I could to make it down the backstretch without seeing a single person to my left.

Success.

I made it off the backstretch alone, with no signs or sounds of anyone else. I rounded the turn, still shredding up the track underneath me, driving over each hurdle as they popped up, one at a time.

The final stretch.

Still, no one was on the inside of my lane. *This is beautiful.*

It *was* beautiful, until my foot clipped the last hurdle leading into the straightaway. That was the time I realized something: there is an element that is even more stubborn than me: wood. Thankfully, it split in half, allowing me to continue running, but not before ripping a gash open on the left knee of my trail leg.

I ignored the pain and drove through the finish line, never seeing a single person in the process. I heard Mima and Papa screaming my name, louder than usual, presumably because I had a trail of blood highlighting my left sock.

I emptied from the track, and Coach Alim congratulated me on the race. "You posted the best time of the day, Gail. Great job!" He looked down at my knee. "Yikes. That's a good one. Get that cleaned up. You earned it today."

Mima and Papa met me at the gate and bandaged me up.

"You know, Gail," Mima said, "I like the hurdles, but maybe you're better suited for the shorter one. So you don't have to worry about hitting any."

I smiled as Papa placed a kiss upon my head.

# CHAPTER 9

"Oh, oh, oh. I got a question!" screams a boy in the front.

"Willis, please," says Mrs. Stephens.

"It's okay. What's the question, Willis?" I ask, leaning down to meet him at eye level.

"Can I be your boyfriend?"

The class erupts in laughter.

"I already have a boyfriend, Willis. But you can be my friend."

"Naw, I wanted to be the boyfriend. Sorry."

"That's enough, Willis," says Mrs. Stephens, frustrated. "Does anyone else have a question for Miss Devers?"

A hand goes up in the middle. "Stand up, Veronica, and ask away," says Mrs. Stephens."

"How did you finally get into the other races?"

"Well, later that year, Coach Alim decided to try me in three more events. The one hundred sprint, one hundred hurdles, and the long jump. You see, in the San Diego county championships, you could only compete in four events. So, he thought I'd have a good shot of helping us win the state title, especially since Phedra was ranked second in the state behind me in the three hundred meter hurdles."

"So, tell us how it went. Please, please, please!" Veronica says.

# CHAPTER 10

"Okay, here's the strategy going in," Coach Alim said, pulling the van into the parking lot early that Saturday morning. "Gail, if you can place in the top three, and Phedra, if you just qualify for the finals — which I'm sure you will — we should have a real chance at winning this thing," he said mildly. As if it'd be that simple.

But I didn't question him one bit, seeing as though he was the coach and I was the athlete. What did I know about scoring, placing, and point systems? I was here to run, and that's what I planned on doing.

I remember that morning as if it was yesterday. The sun beat down on our necks as we went into our basic warm-up laps, performing drills and such. The dew nipped at our heels as we sprinted across the field adjacent to the track. The clouds rolled through every now and then, to provide a sliver of shade from the heat that would eventually catch up with every athlete there. San Diego had a dry heat that ate at you slowly, and dangerously. Before you knew it — if you were not careful — you could have easily collapsed from dehydration. So, Phedra and I stayed as hydrated as possible, carrying endless bottles of water in our sacks.

When we finished, we took shelter underneath the bleachers, and rolled out a blanket to lie down on, and elevated our feet on our sacks. Headphones completed the routine – playing my favorite Christian music – which blocked out the aimless chatter and helped me sink into the moment.

A few hours rolled by, and the muffled sound of the stadium announcer broke through the shielding headphones. I took them off to hear.

I knew the time had come.

It was race time.

The short hurdles would be first, followed by the one hundred. This was quite a double to take on, knowing full well that I'd be tired from the hurdles. My only hope was that the preliminaries would be spaced out a good bit to allow for recovery; with all the heats and set up time, I was confident I'd be able to get my bearings. The key would be to save enough for the finals, Coach Alim had said last night.

Still, there was the long jump to contend with, which made everything all the more a laughable mess. The real problem I had to deal with was not having anything to compare the experience to. The county meet wasn't that competitive, with only a handful of the girls even coming close. The regional was more of a challenge and one girl in particular – Evadnie Simms – pushed me to the finish line in the hundred. I was able to out-lean her at the tape. Coach Alim said it was the worst start I had all season, and if I thought of trying that here, I'd be left behind by the entire pack.

But things would be much different here. The unknowns from all over California would be showing up, probably just coming off their personal best times, filled with adrenaline and enthusiasm. Joyce Thompson would be here. She and Evadnie are both friends from the old neighborhood. They weren't too happy with me staying at Sweetwater – predominantly Black, Somoan, and Mexican – when they transferred to Douglas Turner High, which was mostly black. Both schools were in the general vicinity, but I had already made a good amount of friends where I was so I decided to stay put. Besides, Parenthesis played football there and I didn't want to leave him, no matter how annoying he was. I even adopted a new nickname, courtesy of Parenthesis: "Baby PD," for Parenthesis Devers.

Joyce didn't do so well at the regionals, claiming her blocks slipped at the start of the hurdles, but she was still able to sneak in and qualify for the state. She'd be here and she'd be hungry.

I loaded into the starting blocks and did my best not to think about the long day ahead of me.

"Take one race at a time," Mima had said yesterday, reminding me that all I could do was my best.

"Get set," the starter said.

My hips rose.

The gun fired.

I popped up out of my blocks like I was shot from a cannon. Midway through the race, I realized that no one was in my periphery, and began to shut it down and cruised through the tape. I wasn't sure if it was the sound of cheering that brought me back to the moment, or the evil glare I received from Evadnie on her way down to the starting line, but I felt a wave of relief wash over me nonetheless.

I jogged back down and slid my sweat pants back on to relax before the start of the hurdles. The long jump would follow and later, the long hurdles.

The day went by pretty fast, surprisingly, with me posting my best jump ever in the long jump on my second try. Coach Alim was content with me making the finals with that one, so I didn't jump anymore, although the temptation to put one out there needled at the back of my mind. The three hundred hurdles went even smoother, with me only needing to run the backstretch hard to put the competition away. Joyce finished the day with the fastest qualifying time in the hurdles, and although I didn't meet up with either her or Evadnie in the races, I was the slightest bit apprehensive for what was to come later that night.

"Okay, Gail, it looks like Phedra is going to make it into the finals for the three hundred meter hurdles. That means we have a real good shot of winning this thing, as long as you place first or second in each race and..." he paused and ran his finger down a sheet of wrinkled paper in his hands before finishing, "...somewhere between fourth or fifth in the long jump. Although, I think you'll do better than that. Okay?"

"Okie dokie, Coach," I said.

I scanned the bleachers for Mima and Papa, before retiring for the afternoon to our little palette. Mima caught my eye immediately, as if she could sense I was looking for her. She offered me a wave and kiss. Papa, not so much; too busy listening to the other parents about who would win. Surely he was bragging on his little girl too. I waved back and headed to my hideout where Phedra was keeping things safe. Phedra, my teammate— the only person to share in the excitement of representing Sweetwater with me that day. It was too bad that her senior year would be wasted on such an anti-climactic event if we were to come in second, or worse, *even*. As I squatted down beside her, I gave a thumbs-up before reclining to the sanctuary of my headphones. In my head, I made a silent promise to send her off with a bang.

When the announcer's voice boomed back over the stadium speakers, I was awakened from my daze, and came to a sitting position. Phedra was already up standing at the edge of the bleachers, listening to the announcements. I joined her.

"You didn't miss anything. He's was just going over the lane assignments for the finals." She flashed me a notepad. "I wrote down yours."

"Thanks," I said.

"Looks like you have either lane four or five for most of them. You'll be jumping third in the long jump."

"Great. That should give me enough time to get back to the sprints and be rested for the three hundred hurdles."

She nodded. "I'll be there, waiting." Her voice quieted as she looked at me. Her eyes dropped to the ground and then went back up to me. "Gail, you've been great this year. The best teammate I could ask for. Don't feel, by any means, that you have to kill yourself out there for me."

I shook my head. "Not another word. I do this because I have to."

"You have to? For who?"

"For God, and the gifts He has given me. Nothing more. Winning is just the piece that drives me. I hate losing, so it makes all the practice and hard work that much sweeter. Don't worry; we'll be there in the end." I gave her a pat on the back.

"The next event: The one hundred meter hurdles. Track time is six-thirty. Race time is seven o'clock," the announcer said.

Phedra looked at me. The softness of her normally slanted Latino eyes were now replaced by something much more rigid and firm—almost angry. "You're up. Go get 'em."

I nodded. "Okie dokie."

My warm-up flashed by, and before I knew it, they were calling for me at the starting line. Coach Alim met me there, wrenching his hands together something awful. A wave of nervousness registered in my core and flushed all over my body, down into my fingertips. "Okay, Gail, remember. You need to get a good start. No, I mean: a *great* start. And then there's the drive phase. Punch with your arms." He paused to demonstrate. "And then, as you enter cruising speed —"

"Coach," I said, cutting him off. "I know. I got this. They're calling for me."

Coach Alim panned around, and then gave an audible swallow. "Okay. Yeah, right," he sighed.

I turned and jogged out to the starting line, setting my blocks. Lane five for me, with Evadnie alongside me on four.

"So, looks like we meet again, Devers," Evadnie hissed. "Too bad you have all those events to run. I know how that could take a lot out of you."

"Don't you have two other races as well?"

"Yeah, but I didn't have to run on the legs of the four hundred relays. We have *teammates* who could do that. And the two hundred isn't my race. I'm just trying to get points."

I smiled, standing. "Well, best to you."

"Best to you?" she sneered. "Between Joyce and me, you don't have a chance, especially with all that you've done. Let me know how the back of my jersey looks when we finish."

There's something about smack talking that is very odd. It either makes you feel very light or very disgusted. I'm either overcome with joy or anger, depending on who is delivering it. In this case, I leaned more to the side of joy, and did my best to hold back a laugh, knowing Evadnie only mouthed off like that when she was afraid.

I fed off of it.

Ignoring her last words, I slid off my sweats and got ready to put on a show.

"Runners, take your marks," the starter said.

I squatted, placed my palms on the ground in front of me, and began to walk my feet backwards, loading into the blocks silently. I gave one last look down the track before dropping my head, and waited.

"Get set," the starter said.

My hips rose.

Boom!

The gun sounded more like a canon that night, as the shot echoed into the recesses of the stadium. This time, Evadnie ripped out of the blocks first, along with a girl to my right in lane six. It took a minute for me to register that I had some work to do, but before long, my instincts took over and I began to eat up the track in front of me. I felt my knees elevating faster and faster with each step, as I bounded off the rubberized surface. No longer was Evadnie out in front of me, but we were even, both of us, chasing the girl to my right.

*Where did she come from?* I thought.

It was one thing to lose to Evadnie, but another thing to finish second to someone else; especially someone who

I hadn't even accounted for. With about thirty meters left, I realized that Evadnie had become a distraction. I placed way too much of my focus on her and allowed others to become a threat. Coach Alim's words came barreling back into my head: "You can't count anyone out of a race. You have to always remember to stay in your lane and only do what you need to do. Recall your training, and your talent will pull you through."

I did just that.

Focusing on my stride, I realized that I relied way too much on my legs to accelerate. I quickly began to pump my arms as fast as I could. My legs followed, chipping away at the slight lead by the girl in six, Evadnie now a shadow in my left periphery.

Faster, faster.

As we closed in on the finish line, I could see the girl in six tightening up.

We were now even. All that was left to do was lean at the tape.

Flashbulbs went off, blinding me slightly as I dipped my shoulder and turned my head to the camera. Slowing down to a slight jog, I turned to watch the scoreboard. My eyes beat back and forth between the judges and the scoreboard.

Finally, my name registered in lights. First place, with Evadnie bringing up third.

Immediately, I jumped for joy and looked into the stands for Mima and Papa. They waved and shouted my name. Coach Alim stood by the fence, and pointed at his stopwatch. "A new personal best, Gail," he said.

I didn't have time to find out what it was, because the hurdles were next, with only the boys' hundred meter separating us. I jogged back down to grab a bottle of water.

Phedra came up behind me. "Great job, Gail. Take a seat and rest."

I took her advice and sat next to my things, catching my breath. Evadnie walked by, unable to look me in the eyes. The boys finished their race and before I know it, the meet staff was busy on the track, setting up the hurdles. I stood to my feet, and took a couple of runs over the first one to calm my nerves.

"Hey, Devers, nice run. Hope you have something left so this isn't too easy?" asked Joyce.

*Another nervous one.*

I couldn't be too confident, though. The one thing about hurdling that sets it apart from any other race is that anyone can win at any given time, because no matter how fast you are, you must cross every barrier. One loss in concentration, and that's it.

The barriers were set before us, and the starter called us to line up in our respective lanes. This time, I drew four and Joyce was in five. My time in the semi-final was just a hair's breadth faster than hers. There was no doubt about it: this was my hardest test of the night.

"Runners, take your mark," the starter said.

I loaded in the blocks, just like before.

"Get set," he continued.

My hips rose.

Boom!

I exploded from the blocks. My best start ever. No Joyce. No anyone.

Boom, boom!

*Three shots?* I thought.

"Come back, ladies. We have a jump in lane four," he said.

*A jump in lane four? That's me,* I thought.

"You only get one more jump, Four. After that, you're gone," he said mildly.

I heard a small chuckle, over to my right, and turned to see who it was. Joyce, sporting a smile as long as the entire track.

*I'll wipe that smile off, even if I have to stay in the blocks.*

Now, Joyce had complete advantage over me, because the false start was only charged to the person who jumped. So, I had to be extra careful, while the other seven could take chances. And Joyce knew it as well as I did.

My race would have to be perfect after the start to beat her.

"Runners, take your mark."

I knelt and took a deep breath, rolling my feet back into the blocks.

"Get set."

My hips rose.

Boom!

This time Joyce was out like a light, snapping over the first hurdle before I could even get my lead leg across it. I pulled my trail leg under my armpit, and punched as hard as I could to drive it to the track. I began to drive harder, focused on only my lane and my hurdles. Crossing five, Joyce and I were even, but I was in a rhythm.

Lead, tuck, snap, drive.

The words played on repeat in my head, as I thought of nothing else but getting to that finish line before the entire field. The last hurdle came up, and I took a quick breath with the thought of beating Joyce. My worst fears clouded my headspace.

My lead leg clipped the hurdle.

Immediately, the rest of the field pulled even in my periphery; Joyce to my right, lanes two and three to my left.

Five steps left to close it out.

My mind spun to the last bit of coaching. *Drive, drive, drive.*

I leaned.

Flashbulbs ignited around us.

The officials made a mad dash for the video, stopwatches in hand.

My heart raced at the thought of losing. Phedra, Coach Alim, Mima, and Papa.

*How could I let them down with my momentary lapse of focus?*

In what seemed like forever, the decision finally came.

"In a photo finish, the runner from Sweetwater is declared the winner," one announcer said.

This time, instead of running, I collapsed into a squat with a long sigh of relief. *One jump left, one race to go.*

# CHAPTER 11

I'm cut off by the sound of the school bell.

"That's it for now, children," says Mrs. Stephens.

"But what about the rest of the track meet? Did you win?" Veronica asks.

"Well, I won the three hundred hurdles, and came in second in the long jump. But as a team, we finished second," I say.

"Aww, man. That stinks. But you did so well," says Veronica.

"I know. But it's not always about winning. Sometimes it's about the effort you put forth, and the lessons you learn in the process."

Veronica's not convinced. "What did you learn from losing?"

I smile. "Just that: winning isn't everything, and to stay focused at all times."

Mrs. Stephens gathers the children for their teacher, and walks me to the front office. "Thank you so much, Gail, for coming by. The kids had an amazing time, and I'm sure *they*, as well as I, really enjoyed your stories. You have to come back someday."

"I will. It was a blast."

# PART II: DRIVE PHASE

# CHAPTER 12

It's midday Tuesday afternoon by the time I pull up to the *Boys and Girls Club of Atlanta*. I check my phone for messages, just before shutting down the engine.

"No calls from Chelan," I whisper.

With that said, I feel sure that this must be the place. I glance over to the front door. Judging by the line outside, I'm not wrong. The parking lot serves as nothing more than a reservoir for catching the crowd bursting from within. Today, I'll be speaking to a little over a hundred children and young adults. Questions can come from anywhere and can be about anything.

If you're not careful, you can be overwhelmed. That trepidation brings with it a fair share of mistakes, trip-ups, and misspoken words. My perfectionist personality cries out: "No, no," colliding against my spirit of humility. So, I grab hold of the car door, take a deep breath, and step out on to the pavement. Upon my approach, a few kids turn and take notice, pointing and screaming my name. Before long, their words mix together with the rest of the crowd in a symphony of loud noise as they approach me.

A young girl runs up to me and hugs me around my waist. "Miss Devers, you're really here," she says. I freeze in my tracks.

A young woman runs up behind her, and takes hold of her hand. "Donna, baby, let go of Miss Devers. She needs to go inside." The woman gives me a look of disbelief. "I'm so sorry. She's a huge fan of yours."

"It's quite all right," I assure her.

"Back up, people," I hear a man say through the noise of the crowd.

I turn to match the voice with the face. "Frank Sanchez?" I ask.

He greets me with an open hand. "Gail Devers. Great to finally meet you in person. We've spoken so much over the phone."

We shake. "Thank you."

He turns and gestures me towards the doors. "Right this way. We have a room set up for you already." He waves his hands at the crowd. "Please, please, everyone. You will all have a chance to meet Miss Devers, but right now, I need to get her inside."

The crowd responds, parting like the Red Sea. After making it inside the building, Frank escorts me through the hallway of onlookers, and safely to a vacant room just off the main gym.

"Here is where we will have you sit until everyone is ready. The press is already here, waiting for you, and the small podium is where you will get a chance to speak and answer questions." He snaps his finger. "Also, the small shipment of books we ordered arrived yesterday and will be available at the end for you to sign."

"Excellent. Thank you for hosting this," I say.

"No problem. We love to have celebrities such as yourself come by and speak to the youth of our neighborhoods. It gives them hope for a brighter tomorrow. The pleasure is all ours. Can I get you something to drink?"

I raise my bottle of water. "I'm good."

Frank eyes the door anxiously and walks over to peer out. "I'm going to step out and will start to allow everyone to come inside. Once we get everyone situated, I'll introduce you and bring you out."

I nod. "Okie dokie."

Moments later, I can hear Arnie's voice resonating above the murmurs of the crowd. We have our audience. I stand and take in a deep breath. My nerves begin to wane.

There's nothing like the feeling of adrenaline pouring through your veins. Sure, stepping out into a stadium of sixty thousand people and running down the track is one thing, but public speaking is quite a beast in its own right.

I only started doing it after I retired, from the urging of my husband, Mike. He's forever the businessman. But he understands the responsibility of fame. Capitalizing on my platform is more than just about making money; it's about reaching people and touching them in a special way. I know that without my gifts, I may have never had a chance like this, ever. So, as nervous as I may be at times, I stay committed.

Frank beckons me out, and I join him on the makeshift stage. A sea of people greets me with a standing ovation, and I bow. "Thank you."

"Ladies and gentlemen, I give you: Gail Devers," says Frank as he backs away from the podium.

I step to the microphone. "Thank you for having me. It is such a pleasure to be here. You all overwhelm me, and I am so grateful for all the love and support through the years, and even up 'til now. My career has granted me the opportunity to touch so many abroad, but there is nothing like coming home to the community and sharing my experiences with people such as you. So, with that in mind, I offer you all the chance to ask me any questions you may have."

Frank cuts in. "If anyone has a question for Miss Devers, please, stand, raise your hand, and when we call upon you, say your name, and speak up as loud as you can."

A hand immediately rises in the front row, and I see that it's connected to a young boy. I point at him, and he stands. "My name is Robby Jordan. I wanted to know how you got started running, and when did you know you were going to be a star?"

"That's a great question, Robby. I wasn't really sure how far I was going to go with this whole track thing until my senior year in high school. I had just led our team to the San Diego conference championship the week before competing in four events, and was back on the track, gearing up for the state meet."

# CHAPTER 13

"Gail, there are some people here to see you," Coach Alim said as I finished my last set of hundred meter wind sprints.

I looked over his shoulder to find two men standing behind him. I caught my breath, and walked over to them. "Hello."

"Gail Devers, right?" the one man on the right asked.

"Yes," I replied.

"You, young lady, put on quite a show last week at the conference meet. Four events, and I heard you only warmed up once," said the one on the left.

I shot a look over to Coach Alim. He smiled guiltily. "Thank you. That's right. But if you don't mind me asking, who are you?"

The man on the left looked shocked at my forwardness. He reached inside his pocket and pulled out a card. "I'm Coach Jenkins, head track and field coach of UCLA." He pointed to the man on his left. "And this is Coach Martin, head of sprints and jumps. Coach Homer Smith, one of the football coaches, was out here two weeks ago, meeting with your high school's star football player, James Primus. He mentioned your name to Coach Smith. Said you had all kinds of talent. Coach Smith relayed the message to me, and we took a peek at you last week at the conference meet. That was spectacular."

"Thank you," I said.

"Gail," interjected Coach Martin. "Athletes like you come only once in a blue moon. We'd love to recruit you to come to UCLA on a full scholarship. California has always had talent, and we'd find it quite a shame if you took that kind of talent out of the state. You can run, compete, and get an education right here in your own backyard."

His eyes widened in a way that made me feel more like a trophy than a person. I had come to get used to it, though. Coaches Martin and Jenkins weren't the first to have approached me. Dozens more had started to step forward as my senior year churned right along. After going undefeated all year in the one hundred meter hurdles, and having broken the state record, it became kind of hard not to attract *that* kind of attention.

I took Coach Jenkins' card and nodded. "Thank you. Sounds interesting." The idea of staying close to home was more than attractive, with Evadnie already signed to go to USC and Joyce choosing San Diego State, my choices were somewhat limited.

"We'd love to have you come out to take a tour of the campus if you'd like," said Coach Martin. "Coach Alim has our contact information and a packet for you to look over."

"Great," I added.

"We'll leave you to your practice, Gail," said Coach Jenkins. He tipped his ball cap and shook Coach Alim's hand. "Talk soon, Coach."

"Talk soon," said Coach Alim.

We watched them load into their truck and pull off. "What do you think, Gail?" asked Coach Alim.

My eyes darted to the card. "I'm not sure yet."

"Well, you have time. The state meet is this weekend, and you still have Junior Trials coming up later in the month. But UCLA is a great school. They are getting some fantastic talent out there. I'd say, if you were asking me, that it's at least worth a visit."

"At least," I repeated.

Two weeks went by, and after leading my team to a state title and two more records, Mima and Papa accompanied me on my visit to UCLA.

The school was nothing less than stunning. Tall buildings met long, paved walkways that connected with oceans of the greenest grass I'd ever seen. The sports facilities were immaculate, housing state-of-the-art equipment and weights. Coach Jenkins toured us around the campus for over an hour, and by the time we finished, I'd made up my mind.

"So, what do you think, Gail?" asked Mima.

"I think I like it," I said staring back into her proud eyes. "I think I'm going to be a Bruin."

Coach Jenkins smiled. "Welcome home, Gail. Coach Martin will put a packet together for you and bring it by your home sometime next week before the US Junior Olympic trials." He shook my hand. "Run hard. We'll see you in the fall." He looked over to Papa and shook his and Mima's hands as well.

With my commitment to UCLA signed and sealed, I focused on what was next: the US Junior Nationals. The best of the best sixteen-to-nineteen-year-olds in the entire country would be competing, vying for only two spots per event. Coach Alim elected to enter me only in the one hundred meter dash and the one hundred meter hurdles. I was somewhat relieved at the news, because the season had gone on longer than expected.

That Saturday morning, on the way to the trials, Papa got a phone call. His face dropped as the voice on the other line chattered away. Papa looked over at me in the rearview mirror, one hand on the wheel, the other clutching his phone. He shot a look to Mima too, who was riding beside him.

"What is it, Papa?" I asked.

"Okay, thank you. We will discuss this and get back to you," Papa said, hanging up the phone.

"What is it? " I repeat.

"It's UCLA, baby." Papa sighed heavily. "That was Judy Holland, the athletic director of UCLA. Seems that the coach and the staff were let go."

"Let go," repeated Mima.

Papa studied me closely in the rearview mirror. "Yeah, something about the school wanting to go another way in lieu of their losing record."

It was the first time in my life that I actually can attest to the feeling of your heart stopping. For the few seconds that mine did, my body felt numb.

*What will I do now?* I thought.

"Judy promised that you have the option to leave if you like, Gail, and attend another college. The decision is up to you." He must've noticed my ghostly stare, and called out to me in a loud voice, "Gail."

This started my heart again. "Yes, Papa?"

"What do you think, baby?" he asked. "I hate to spring news like this on you all of a sudden, but there will undoubtedly be other coaches at this meet. Maybe they still have a few spots available on their teams."

"Maybe some money left over. But I'm sure the full rides are used up," I said.

"Gail, they can make room for you; I'm sure of it," chimed Mima.

I slumped back in my seat and watched the highway drift by in slow motion.

When we finally arrived at the stadium, the idea of competing was a mere whisper in my mind.

*How could I, anyway?* I thought.

There were bigger decisions at stake than taking first place and making a team. Mima and Papa deserved to not worry about me getting into college. Parenthesis had made it on a partial football scholarship, with my parents footing the rest. I couldn't bring a burden of tuition on them now.

I felt both depressed and dejected. It would take everything in me to do my best today. I had to. If I didn't, any chance of making it into college would fall apart.

As we walked to the track, my mind cleared and two objectives merged together like ink on paper. Winning today and crushing my competition could secure both Mima and Papa's finances, and my college future.

Just as I had made up my mind, Papa was approached by another man wearing a Bruins T-shirt, shorts, shades, and a pack around his waist. He introduced himself, and shook Papa's hand. From the distance, neither Mima nor I could hear the conversation.

"Who is that, Mima?" I asked.

"I don't know, baby." She rested her hand on my shoulders. "Let's find a spot in the stands. Your father will find us, I'm sure."

I followed Mima into the stands and helped her secure a spot right on the end, close to the finish line. Coach Alim arrived and waved me down to the field.

*I wonder if he knows about the bad news?*

"Gail, I have your numbers and your lane assignments," he said as I reached him at the starting line.

"Did you hear the news, Coach?" I asked.

He expelled a gust of wind from his mouth. "Yes, I did. Your father told me. But, all is not lost. I think you're going to be okay."

"How's that?" I asked.

"See that man over there?" Coach Alim said, pointing across the field. "The one with the dark shades on and the satchel around his waist?"

"Yeah, the one with the Bruins shirt on," I said.

"He's the new interim Coach for UCLA."

"Really." I look over at Coach Foster. "Do you know anything about him?"

"Well, I hear he's a tough coach. He was an assistant and was handed the job when everyone left. Come with me, I'll introduce you to him."

We cut across the field and stopped in the general vicinity of the new coach next to the jumpers' warm-up area.

"Come on, Dax. You can do better than that. What are you trying to do, embarrass yourself?" he yelled at a boy running into the jumping pit.

*Is that supposed to be my new coach?*

"Coach Kersee!" called Coach Alim.

Coach Kersee turned around with a scowl. His face faded to a half smile when he saw me. He walked over to us.

"Coach Alim, good to see you. This must be Devers," he said.

"Good to see you, too." Coach Alim smiled at me. "This is our little star."

Coach Kersee bent over a bit and looked me dead in the eyes. "How are you, Devers?"

"I'm fine."

"Listen, all these girls out here are trying to be where you are right now. But they can't, because you already occupy that spot. I've seen you run. You're a star," Coach Kersee affirmed.

Like he was going to say anything else.

"Really?" I asked.

Coach Kersee turned away and barked something at another jumper on their approach down the runway. "You might as well go back home." He looked over at me. "You see her over there?"

I followed his finger to another female athlete on the side of the track performing a hamstring stretch. "Yeah."

"Well," he quickly glanced over in her direction and then turned back to me, "she is here trying out for the Olympic trials. She redshirted her senior year at UCLA. You could easily be in her same spot one day. Don't doubt it for a second. If you come to UCLA, you'll see." His eyes peer down at me over the top of his shades. "Mark my words."

# CHAPTER 14

"So, long story short, I medaled at the meet in both the hurdles and the hundred, and kept my commitment to UCLA."

"Any regrets?" asks Robby.

"None that I know of," I add with a smile.

Another hand flies up behind his. This time, a girl stands before we can even offer. Her teeth beam through a wide smile that crowds her ears. "My name is Janet Jones and I want to know how you go about fighting peer pressure?"

My eyes flash over to Frank. He meets me with a nod that indicates he, just like me, is delighted to answer such a question. The kids at the Boys and Girls Clubs are in dire need of role models. Most times, they are served to the influences of the streets and their peers instead, only to wither under the pressure of being cool or hard. Tough decisions breed only loss in the long run.

"Janet, I'll share a conversation with you that my brother and I had, right before he went off to college. I remember him sitting on the front step of our home, watching the sun drop over the horizon. The rays of red, orange, and pink blanketed the blue sky in a palette of color I'd never seen before, so I joined him.

"We sat on the porch that day. Shoulder to shoulder, silent. Parenthesis sighed heavily and dropped his head."

# CHAPTER 15

"Gail," Parenthesis said. "I'm going away next week and expect you to stay strong."

My eyes found the glare of the sun as it blazed over the horizon. "Yes, I know."

"Well, you better, or I'll make sure to come back and put a hurting on you." He shoved me with his elbow. It was a gentleness I had never before seen in him. It was like he was someone different. So much so that I was tempted to ask if he could send my brother back soon, so I could have a one last decent conversation. But I refrained.

"Whatever," I replied softly.

"Truth is, I worry more about myself with peer pressure than I do about you."

My voice cracked, "Really?"

"You've always been *Gail,* no matter what people said or thought about you." He finally looked over at me. "Kind of a weird," he joked.

I shoved him again. "Not weird." I search for the right word. "Just unique."

Parenthesis shook his head. "Unique...right," he said in a hushed tone.

There was something hiding beneath all those thick layers of *older brother* skin he had fashioned all the years I'd known him. The quiver in his voice was a dead giveaway. It was less the sense of him trying to hide something, and more like he was beckoning me to delve deeper and reveal some truth he wanted to impart to me.

"You sound a little *weird* yourself," I said. "What's up, big bro?"

"It's nothing. It's just, nowadays, I feel like I'm the younger brother. I feel the pressure of life, friends, college, and even the responsibilities of becoming a man weighing down on me."

I eased my arm around his back and cupped his shoulder with my hand. "You'll be fine. All you have to do is your best. Papa told me a long time ago that his father drilled into his kids this one truth: 'Be the best you that you can be. Nothing more or less.'"

"You're quoting old men now? I must really be the younger brother."

"Think about it. As long as you put forth your best efforts, you will never have anything to feel bad about.

Mima and Papa always encourage us to try hard, but never to the point that our passion turns bitter."

"And how did you avoid the peer pressure?"

I shrugged my shoulders. "The truth?"

He nodded.

"I really don't know. I can't say I really ever had any. People see me as they want to. Most of the time, I'm seen as more of a leader than a follower, so no one really tried to sway me to do what the crowd did. I walked at my own rhythm. My own pace. Try to listen to the voice in your head that talks to you and tells you that you are meant to be more than just another kid from the street."

Parenthesis' face wrinkled. "You are weird."

"Whatever. The girl with the all-white long socks and two French braids keeps it real. Don't have time to be fake."

"Right."

I gave him one last shake and squeezed him close to my side. "You'll be fine, bro. You're talented in so many things: football and school. You're going to shine. And I'll be here rooting for you every step of the way." I gave a wink. "Like a good little sister should."

Parenthesis flashed me a smile-filled smirk. "Like a good one should." He gave me a hug. "Thanks, sis."

# CHAPTER 16

"So, where I may not know exactly the best way to stand up against peer pressure, I do know one thing. You've got to make a stand and deicide on what kind of person you are going to be, and how you will live that out," I say.

Janet sits, spouting out a sharp, "Thank you."

A voice catches my attention from the left. This time, it's male, and attached to one of the reporters. "Hello, Miss Devers. My name is Darius, from the local Atlanta evening news. First and foremost, congratulations on your fabulous track career."

"Thank you, Darius," I reply.

"A lot has been reported on how Grave's disease took such a toll on your life, but you've been such an example of perseverance throughout, and your story is quite inspirational, if nothing else. But, what has not been documented at length are the smaller details emanating from the time you started your track career in college, up until that day you were formally diagnosed. I was wondering if you could take a little time and walk us through those experiences, if you wouldn't mind sharing."

I swallow. "Certainly. It was late fall of nineteen eighty-six, when I finally started my official practice sessions with the rest of the team. Since landing on the UCLA campus, I couldn't avoid the stir my arrival had sparked."

# CHAPTER 17

"How do you do it, Gail?" Monica asked.

I adjusted the strap of my book bag over my shoulder. "Do what?"

"You know," she started, looking around the cafeteria before sitting. "Act like you don't hear them chatting."

I sat down next to her, and panned my eyes slowly around the room. "I don't hear anything."

"Whatever, Gail. You know what I mean. Everyone wants to know how things are going to be this year with the team, now that Coach is gone."

"Well, don't we still have a coach?"

"Coach Kersee? Word has it he's kind of crazy. It was a huge risk for the athletic director to hand the job over to him like that."

"It didn't seem to stop you from coming on board."

"Truth be told, I might have reconsidered if they hadn't told me so late. I just didn't have time to find another option. Don't get me wrong. I think Coach Kersee knows his stuff. I'm just not so sure on how much is running loose in that head of his."

"I think he knows his stuff. Still, all that yelling is going to get old pretty quick. The only thing that will get me over it is winning."

"Amen to that." With her fork, she stirred something on her plate that resembled spaghetti. "I'm glad I have you for a roommate."

"Same here."

Finally, Monica gave up trying to put another bite in her mouth. She dropped her fork and chugged down a glass of water. "I can't do it. Listen, I think I'm going to head to the training room a little early and get some work done on my shins. They're killing me. I'll meet you over there."

"Okie dokie."

Monica left the table and my eyes darted around the room. No one even acknowledged my presence. "Talking about me," I whispered with a laugh. "Why would anyone be worried about what I think?"

I finished off the last of my sandwich and headed over to the track. Running on grass had been something new to me, but Coach Kersee swore that we needed to put our bodies to the test early, and leave the track alone for the moment. So, I did my best to avoid the soreness by icing down after practice and heating up before.

By the time I arrived for practice, the training room was packed. Athletes from all teams were sardined together, with football taking full priority, and basketball and baseball coming next. If I had to take a guess, I'd have said that track athletes fall somewhere towards the bottom of the totem pole when it comes to sports. But Parenthesis warned me about that during his first semester, saying that football ruled because they brought the most money to the school.

Since none of the trainers bothered to pay me any attention, I grabbed two heating packs and found an open spot on the carpet. Resting the packs on my hamstrings, I leaned back, closed my eyes, and zoned out to my headphones.

I felt the presence of someone hovering over me, and opened my eyes.

"Hey, there," a friendly face said. A young male, clean shaven, with bright brown eyes casted a wide smile at me.

I answered with a, "Hello," of my own, and hoped he'd leave it at that.

"Getting in a little rest time before practice, huh?"

"Yeah. Aren't you on the men's team?" I asked.

He slid over to the side, and sat next to me. "Yeah. My name's Jared Dobery. Nice to meet you. I run the hundred."

It was then that I heard the thickness of his island accent, especially when he said the word *hundred*.

"I'm Gail. I run a little bit of everything."

"Don't we all? I only desire to run one thing. But I know with Coach Kersee, that's impossible. He uses the entire track to train his athletes."

"Well, I'm used to that. My old Coach came up with some crazy methods of getting me to run faster. So, I think I'm up to the challenge."

Jared paused. "I'm sure you are," he said in a low tone.

For some stupid reason, I felt my cheeks begin to flush. That was when I determined that the hot pack had done its job, and quickly stood to return it to the hydrocullator.

"Nice meeting you, Jared," I said, walking away.

Coach Kersee's reputation for craziness was not lost by way of track practices. By the time we hit the indoor season, we'd been through more four hundred and two hundred repeats than I could count, minus a few eight hundred intervals and mile laps, and I was virtually ready to compete in any one of eight races. He'd even gone as far as wearing a pair of roller skates and had us pull him around the track in a harness. Once I'd finishing laughing at the sight of him, I was able to focus. Miraculously, it was one of the better workouts I'd had working the turns. He said I'd need it if I was ever going to be any good at running the last leg of the four hundred relay.

When the spring rolled around, it was time for our first outdoor meet, the Pepsi Challenge. Somehow, I had managed to get myself invited to compete in the women's open hundred meter hurdles, not knowing that both college and professional athletes would be competing. If nothing else, it'd serve as a good barometer to let me know where I stood, or fell, for that matter.

I came to the starting line, and began to take off my sweats. Before I could take off my jacket, I heard Coach Kersee calling out to me from the stands. I tried to wave him off; knowing we'd start the race soon, but he just kept just calling me.

Finally, I ran over to see what he wanted.

"Gail," he said, staring at me over his shades, "I just wanted to tell you this is your first big meet. There are some of the finest runners here." He stopped to observe the competition, and then panned back to me. "Just don't choke!"

"What?" I whimpered, after he turned away and disappeared back into the stands.

I could feel the steam spouting from my ears.

*Was he trying to mess me up? Another crazy tactic to get inside my head?*

I shook off the episode, returned to the start, and waited for the starter to ready the race.

"Runners, take your mark," he said, gesturing to us with his free hand.

I loaded into my blocks, blocking out everything.

"Get set," he continued.

My hips rose as I held my breath. My body froze as a silent hush smothered the stadium. Only the sound of the gun could alert me now.

Boom!

I exploded out of the blocks, so fast, in fact, that I waited for a second gun to go off and hear someone call me back to the starting line, due to a false start. But no such thing happened. I ran across the tape alone, no one within five meters.

Coach Kersee met me in the infield. "Nice job, Gail."

"I may mess up, but I will never choke," I said, floating past him on my way back to the finish line.

He grabbed me by the wrist before I could walk away. "Listen to me. I have to motivate you any way I see fit. You have unlimited potential and I have to tap into it. You need to fear the *Negro* in the stands more than you fear anyone on the track."

"Whatever," I said, snatching my arm away.

From that time on, Coach Kersee never tried to pull anymore mind games with me. I was officially on my way to be relevant in the world of track and field. I won the majority of my races in both the hundred meters and the hundred meter hurdles, along with occasionally competing in the long jump, triple jump, and two hundred. As a team, we were fairly competitive, and our four by one hundred meter relay squad was always near the top three finishers.

Monica, who ran third leg on the relay, was more than just a roommate; she was my friend.

Jackie was the star of the team though, coming back to finish her senior year, and had already become a world-class champion in the heptathlon. She made Coach Kersee a household name. When she graduated, I felt the weight and the focus of the program fall upon my shoulders. And while it wasn't something I shied away from, it certainly wasn't anything I longed for.

Monica took me home with her one weekend our freshman year. I was greeted by a host of folks. Monica's family – her mom and dad, Celeste and Johnny along with sisters Debbie and Dide, and her brother Mike – were very friendly.

"Hello, I'm Gail," I said, shaking his hand.

Mike stepped forward, "Hi, Gail. Mike. This is my girlfriend Carla." She nodded.

"Nice to meet you," I said.

"And this is my *man*, Chris," Monica said.

Chris shook my hand. "Monica's told me a lot about you."

"Is that right, roomie?" I asked.

"Don't worry, all good stuff," Monica replied.

We ate dinner as a family, and I was more grateful to Monica than she'd ever know.

# CHAPTER 18

"When did you get hit with Grave's disease?" Darius asks.

"It must have been right around my senior year in college. I remember it well because it was the Olympic year. I had broken the American record in the hundred meter hurdles while still competing for UCLA, and had also qualified to make the Olympic team in Korea. At that time, no one really paid any attention to female hurdlers because we hadn't finished terribly well in past Olympics. I wanted to change their minds. I had officially turned professional and left college behind. Breaking that American record was a good start. But something happened. All of a sudden, the symptoms of sluggishness and fatigue I had fought over the entire season were beginning to catch up with me.

"Since breaking the record in the hurdles back in May of that year, Coach Kersee thought that maybe I was getting run down and decided to pull me from the hundred meters and let me focus solely on the hurdles. With the Olympic trials set for July, this would give me enough rest to be ready for it. I ended up finishing second, but I did make the team, which is all I really wanted to do. There'd be time to go for first at some other point.

"Problem was, as my Grave's disease was advancing, so were my symptoms. I was beginning to lose weight, and practice became harder and harder. The few meets I competed in between the trials and Korea were embarrassing. I could barely beat anybody. I remember looking at myself in the mirror one day and saying, 'This is not Gail.'

"When I got to Korea, I ran the slowest time I'd ever run, dating back to high school. I was broken. My faith was shattered. When we got back to the States, I was almost ready to hang it up. I stopped going outside a lot, I had lost so much weight and could not explain the way I looked and got tired of the stares. I would go to the Phillips house as a reprieve from the world. Thinking back, I recall this one time going there, I was laid out on the couch, exhausted. Chris and Mike came in and were shocked by my drastic change in appearance. They sat down next to me and in true brotherly fashion started grilling me with questions. Who I'd seen? What did the Doctor say? Did I get a second opinion? Even suggested I go and see someone else. They went on and on. Eventually, my mom came through and saved me, making them leave me alone saying. 'Gail came to visit me, not be lectured by you two!' she'd said. Before they left, they made me promise to schedule more appointments so I could get answers and to keep them posted. I took their advice and started seeing doctors from all over. Finally, in nineteen ninety, after barely competing and going from one doctor to the next and still not getting an answer, I decided to end it all."

# CHAPTER 19

"Okay, Coach Kersee, I have something to give you," I said, standing in front of him in his office.

He peered up at me over his glasses. "What's that?"

"My resignation letter. I'm tired of wasting your time, Bobby. I need to let you work with other athletes and focus on getting them better."

Bobby took the letter and read it. Time stood still as I awaited his response.

Bobby reclined in the chair and held the letter out to me. "Are you serious?" Before I could respond, Bobby ripped the letter in half and stood. "You are one of the strongest people I've ever met in my entire life, and you think that just because you lost a little weight, and your hair is falling out, that you have the right to quit? Come on, Gail. There has to be some way to treat whatever is making you sick."

"But I've tried everything."

"Try some other *everythings* then." Bobby sighed heavily. "You remember what I used to always tell you when you competed in college?"

"What? Don't choke?" I murmured, eyes tearing.

"Well, what I used to always call you."

"A dork?"

He waved his finger at me. "Yeah, that's right. And what would you do when I said that?"

"I'd do my hardest to prove to you that I wasn't a dork."

"Precisely! Now, do the same thing again. Try your hardest, Gail. There will be a spot for you when you get back."

And just like that, in true Bobby Kersee fashion, my resignation was annulled. Bobby had seen something in me the first day he'd met me on that track at the Junior Olympics, and he wasn't going back on it. And because of him, I felt the strength to try again.

The next few months were nothing less than exhausting. I could take the weight and hair loss, but when my eyes starting bulging, I nearly lost it. I felt like a leper. I had to start shopping at this clothing store in LA that had extra small clothes because none of my regular clothes fit me anymore.

Finally, I was diagnosed with Grave's disease. A flood of relief washed over me. It wasn't because I had a peace of mind that I could be cured that made me feel that way. At the time, people knew little to nothing about Grave's disease, so a cure was unimaginable. But it was the sense of comfort I felt about finally *knowing* what was affecting me that reinforced my resolve.

A study into Grave's disease concerning radioactive iodine treatment held some promise, so I tried it. The iodine dampened some of my symptoms and allowed me to return to the track.

"You ain't going to start glowing at night, are you?" joked Bobby.

"No," I replied. "But if I do, I'll be sure to stop by the house and shower you with my new powers."

"Don't do me any favors," said Bobby.

But the iodine held a real side effect other than glowing. One day, while participating in some hurdle drills, Bobby called out to me from the other side of the track.

"Gail, come over here," he said.

I jogged over. "Yeah, Bobby?"

"I need you to take hurdles three and four and spread them out one to two feet apart from where they are now."

I nodded. "Okay, Bobby."

I jogged back over to the other side of the track and started my drills. After five or ten minutes of warming up, Bobby called out to me again. "Gail, what are you doing?"

"Warming up!" I yelled back.

"Weren't you supposed to move the hurdles?"

"No, why?"

"You dork. I asked you that about five minutes ago."

"No, you didn't."

Our shouting match went on for about another minute, with Bobby finally so fed up, threw down his stop watch and made his way over to the hurdles to adjust them himself. "Okay, now. Can you please bring hurdles one and two in closer as well when you get a chance?"

"Sure, Bobby," I said. "Just let me finish putting on my shoes.

Five minutes later, I was doing sprints up and down the backstretch.

Bobby caught up with me. "Gail!" he cried out. His voice sounded morbid; a tone I'd never thought to identify with Bobby. He rested his hands on my shoulders and looked me dead in the eyes. "Do you remember what I asked you to do?"

I paused, considering his words. Bobby wasn't joking or screaming. In fact, it was the most calm I'd ever come to see him in my life, ever. "Wind sprints, right?"

"No, Gail," he said somberly. "I asked you to make the adjustments on the hurdles. Just like I asked you to do before."

"Are you serious? I'm so sorry, Bobby. Let me do it now."

Bobby held on to my shoulders and didn't let me walk away. "Something's happening to your mind, Gail. Maybe it's all this radioactive stuff. You need to get see a doctor."

I went to the doctor the next day. It turned out that Bobby was right, again. One of the adverse side effects of the iodine treatment was memory loss. They started me on another regimen of treatment for the disease. This time, it was only supposed to last for six months. I was more than hopeful. Perhaps now, I could put this all behind me. But what was promised for only six months went on for much, much longer.

# CHAPTER 20

"When did the treatments stop?" asks Darius.

"Never did. I'm still taking a daily regimen to this day," I say.

Another reporter stands, making her way to the microphone. Clearing a handful of hairs from her face, she clears her throat and smiles. "Hello, Gail. Marsha Weathersby, from the Dekalb County Press. You've spoken at length on Grave's disease and the harmful effects it has on people, notwithstanding the toll it had on your career. Can you tell us about your road to recovery?"

"Yes. It wasn't until April of nineteen ninety-one when I truly began to understand the disease more, and was able to adapt my workouts and manage it. My strength began to return, along with my speed, and that brought with it the confidence I was lacking. A few years went by, and suddenly, I was beginning to feel like my old self again on the track. Whatever was stolen from me had returned; I had hopes to make another run at Olympic gold. But more than that, I was so grateful that I had unknowingly become the face and the voice of a misunderstood disease. Now I was able to not just speak about Grave's disease, but also show people that they didn't have to be a prisoner any longer to it. They could set goals and make efforts to win again. Just like me."

# PART III:

# FINDING MY STRIDE

# CHAPTER 21

"Yeah, Mike. I will be sure to call you back when it is over. Bye, babe."

I hang up the phone and slide it into my purse, just as I'm met by a flock of teenagers and younger kids. One boy clings to my wrist on my right, while another grabs my other hand. The site for the track clinic is perfect. Clear blue skies are overhead, sending slivers of light through the clouds that warm my skin. Dark, green layers of thick grass greet my eyes as I step through the gates of the stadium.

"Miss Devers, how does it feel to be both a world champion and an Olympic gold medalist?" asks the boy on my left.

Before I can answer, a loud, booming voice cries out from behind. "Marcus, please allow Miss Devers a chance to breathe before we start with questions."

I turn to find a round, ruddy looking man gesturing for Marcus to obey.

"It's all right," I say.

"Really, Miss Devers, so very sorry. We want to get everyone settled before questions start firing." Marcus goes to the man's side and grabs his leg.

"Sorry, Mr. Slade," says Marcus.

"No problem, buddy." The man looks up at me and offers his hand. "James Slade; a pleasure to meet you. Chelan said you'd be here early and she was not wrong."

I give his hand a shake. "Yeah, that's a habit of mine. I always tried to arrive early for track meets so I'd be prepared. And as it turns out, after twenty-five years of professional competition, old habits die hard."

"No need for apologies; we're just about ready anyway." James looks around the field, as if searching for something he's lost. He fixates on a patch of field just beyond the goal posts of the football field in the center of the track. His hand finds his chin as he focuses. "Over there," he says, pointing. "I want to set up over there. I think it'd be perfect, away from the sun, so it won't stab you in the eye. What do you think, Gail?"

"No problem. Whatever's best for you guys. I just want to make sure the kids have enough room to spread out."

"Now, Chelan sent me the agenda last week, and it says that you want to start with a brief Q & A, then allow the kids to introduce themselves, and follow up with the individual drills, skill performances, and then break for sections with individual coaches." His voice drops off into a whisper. "I assume you'll be monitoring those portions very closely?"

"Yes, of course," I reply.

"Not that I don't trust my staff, but if we could do this on our own, well, we'd do *this* on our own, if you get me?"

"I do. That's what I'm here for."

His smile breaks into his eyes. "Perfect. Then we're all set." He waves at another staff member in the distance. "Ron, round the kids up and take them over to the south side of the field."

It's another fifteen minutes or so of set-up by the team, getting the equipment in place, gathering the kids, separating them into groups and such, before I take my place next to James in front of them.

"Children, parents, and adults alike, thank you so much for coming out today to this very special track clinic. Our host is world-class, Olympic medalist, and track and field legend, Gail Devers. She is so accomplished, and such an amazing inspiration to us all, and we are very much honored to have her here in the city of Dayton." James turns to find me. "So, without further ado, please welcome to the state of Ohio, the amazing Gail Devers."

I'm greeted by a round of applause and step forward with a slight bow. "Thank you all for coming out here today," I say among the noise. When everyone finally quiets down, I speak again. "You all are here because you want something. You want to see the fruit of your efforts end with accomplishing your goals. For some of you, that end game will be winning; lots and lots of winning. And for others, maybe it's just competing at a high level and continuing to drop your times and improving your personal bests each time you step on the track. And that's great.

"But ultimately, what's truly significant is developing the will to be a change agent. To go out into the world and use your gifts to gain attention, and build a platform so that you can share your personal testimonies of triumph, and hopefully inspire others to do the same. That's what I do, and that's why I'm here today. To share my knowledge with you so that you can do the same. Give back to those who are in need, whenever you can. So, in following the agenda for today, I will start out with answering a few questions from the group."

"Can we start with mine?" Marcus calls out.

My eyes find him, perched on the front row to my left.

"Sure, Marcus, let's start with yours. For those who don't know, Marcus asked what it feels like to be both an Olympic and World gold medalist. That's a great question, but first I'd like to start with a personal story that reflects the importance of the word *commitment*. When I was in my last year of college, I got married, and my hope was to have children and a house on the hill with a white picket fence. Things were going well for me, really well on the track, and I felt that nothing could derail me from achieving my goals. Unfortunately, right around the end of my senior year in eighty-eight, after I went on to win the NCAA track and field championship in the hurdles and breaking the American Record, I became sick around the time of the US Nationals qualification rounds for the Olympics in Korea. What is now known to be Grave's Disease went undiagnosed, and the only thing I *earned* that year was a heart full of disappointment and ache.

"My husband couldn't understand what was happening to me, and truly wasn't ready to deal with or accept it. No one was, including myself. So, we went our separate ways, and ultimately divorced three years later."

# CHAPTER 22

"Hey, Gail, how you doing?" Mike asked, leaning against the doorframe of the kitchen in the Phillips home.

I had come by to visit that weekend and we were all sitting around the table. It was my way of taking a break from the track for a while to clear my head. My recent divorce had weighed on me heavily, making it hard to concentrate on something as trivial as running. It was enough to make me quit entirely. That is, until the news I had been anxiously waiting for finally arrived.

"I'm actually doing great. Did you hear the news?"

"Yeah, my mom told me," Mike said, as he pulled up a chair at the table.

"They finally figured out what was wrong with me. I'm not crazy."

"The jury is still out on that one," said Monica, in a joking fashion.

"Ha, ha, very funny," I said. "I mean it. This thing has been hovering over me like a dark cloud and now, finally, I have a reprieve. At least, for a while. Something called Grave's disease."

"I asked if you were all right, but I wasn't really talking about your illness," Mike said. "I was talking about the divorce. You good?"

"I'm fine."

He waved his finger at me. "See there? There's that quick and to the point answer that always hides the real truth, Gail."

"Always hides the truth," I refuted.

"Don't try to play it off; we know you."

"Who knows me?" I huffed and rolled my eyes. "What do you think *you* know about me, mister?"

Mike leaned back, hands in the air. "Ease up," he said with a smile. "I was just being concerned.

## CHAPTER 23

"I continued my close relationship with Monica and her family even became godmother of all three of her and Chris' kids," I say.

"Can you tell me a little more about Grave's disease?" a slender reporter in the back asks.

"What would you like to know?" I ask.

"Well, tell us a little about your daily regimen."

"I take one pill a day, for the rest of my life. I have to go to the doctor several times a year, for routine check-ups. You see, Grave's disease is an autoimmune disease that affects the thyroid, making it enlarge nearly twice its size, making it become overactive. This causes side effects such as muscle weakness, increased heartbeat, disturbed sleep, and irritability. It can also make your eyes bulge. The doctor makes sure to check my thyroid levels to ensure that my medication is doing its job to keep my thyroid in check. The higher the numbers, the less medication I have to take. The lower the number, the stronger the dosage."

"Miss Devers, Miss Devers, I have a question!" screams a boy from the middle section. His missing front teeth cause a slight hissing sound to resonate when he calls my name.

I point to him. "Yes, ask away."

"I want to know if you finished school."

"Actually, I did. My senior year at UCLA was a great one. I qualified for seven events, and finished with three records in the hundred, hurdles, and the triple jump. That year, I also broke the American record for the hundred meter hurdles. I graduated prior to trying out for the United States National Championships. I made the team, but fell short because of the Grave's disease."

The little boy shakes his head slowly from side to side. "If only you knew, huh?"

"If only I knew," I repeat, with a shake of my own. "But that wasn't the only thing that ever kept me off the track. Back in nineteen ninety-one, I remember being home one day and Parenthesis and Tracy were there with me. I woke from taking a nap in the most excruciating pain."

# CHAPTER 24

"Parenthesis, Tracy!" I cried out.

"Gail?!" they replied, from downstairs.

I could make out the sound of their feet crashing up the stairs, as I tried to drown out the pain with my eyes tightly closed. When they entered the bedroom, all I could do was lay back and lift my feet to the sky.

"What is it, Gail?" they asked, now supporting my legs.

Blood dripped from the swollen, cracking skin along the dorsum and plantar aspects of my feet. "I'm not sure," I said, grunting.

"We've got to get you to a doctor. This has been going on now for a couple of days, but this is the worst I've seen it yet."

This time, unlike his previous attempts to convince me to take a day off, I relented and responded only with a silent head nod.

We called Bobby and let him know what was going on, and said we would contact him later with any updates. After returning home from the podiatrist, Parenthesis was slightly enthusiastic about the diagnosis: a major case of athlete's foot. I was less enchanted, fearing that it had to be something more. Never in my entire career had I ever experienced athlete's foot. But even the cases I had witnessed never presented like this.

"This should clear up in no time," said Parenthesis, applying the prescribed medicine over my skin. I stepped out of myself for a moment and time stood still, as I watched my brother have to be strong for *me*. I knew it was hard for him because I had always been the strong one. Looking into his eyes, I could tell deep down inside he was a wreck. In his solitude, he probably let it pour out. But in my presence, he stepped up, trying to lessen my pain like a true big brother.

"Maybe," I said with a hint of doubt.

"Don't you think he knows what he's talking about?"

"Yeah, I do, but after all I've been through, it's harder for me to go with the first diagnosis of something so freaky."

Parenthesis nodded. "I get that. But athlete's foot is common, especially in the track world. Maybe after all you've been through, you've finally earned a break, you know? Be positive."

I smile half-heartedly. "I will."

The next few weeks, things only got worse. My skin continued to peel, especially around my Achilles' tendon, which made it impossible to wear any track shoes or even jog on the balls of my feet. I would be sidelined again.

Frustrated, I returned to the doctor for a follow-up visit and learned that it was indeed more than just a case of Athlete's foot, but actually an inflammatory response of my Grave's Disease, due to a mix of some medicines I was taking and the fluctuations of the weather. There was no way of telling exactly what it was, so I was hospitalized for further assessment. A specialist came on board and prescribed some anti-inflammatory medications to decrease the swelling.

A few days passed, and the swelling began to subside. I was able to finally wear a decent pair of sprint shoes again and returned to the track. Bobby met me at the gate.

He ripped his cap from his head. "Gail, are you out of your mind?"

"No. I'm here to do something. I can't stay in that house another day. It's been weeks, Bobby. Too long. I've got to at least watch."

Bobby cocked his head at me like I was some crazy human puzzle. After taking a deep breath, he turned back to the track. "Okay, I have a stationary bike over there," he said pointing. "You can ride it. I'll script up some interval sets for you to build your endurance and loosen you up. But that's all you can do."

My smile touched my ears. "Okie dokie."

"Don't give me that 'okie dokie' mess, either. You're a world-class sprinter, Gail. But you've got the worst luck I've ever seen. You know that?"

"Just makes for a stronger story to tell one day, Bobby."

Bobby remained quiet, only offering a huff as I passed by. I rode the bike that day for as long as I could stand. But apparently, it did more good for me than I thought. The swelling seemed to improve over night. At home, I got real friendly with one of my favorite shows of all time—I Love Lucy—adding sets of sit-ups and push-ups in between commercial breaks. Another day of rest, and I was back on the track jogging. By the end of the week, sprinting resumed. I felt rejuvenated.

There's nothing as powerful as being deprived of something to make you appreciate it more. To just walk again pain free was the equivalent of what I can only imagine it must be like to walk on air.

It was the sound of my feet tapping in between and over the hurdles as I shot down the track that reinforced my resolve, and made the next few months pass by in a blink. Not before too long, my confidence had returned, and I was ready to move on.

Ready to move beyond the Grave's disease.

Ready to move beyond the hiccups along the way.

And ready to move into the pathway to achieve my dreams.

It was March of nineteen ninety-one – the year of the World's Championship – when I set my sights on gold. I even made a contract with myself. I remember sitting in front of the mirror, repeating the words, "I, Gail Devers, vow to make it back to the track...and win."

And that I did, taking first place at the United States Championships in the hundred meter hurdles. With just a little less than a year of training under my belt, I still hadn't regained my speed, so even placing in the finals of the World Championships would be considered a miracle.

"Now, Gail, I don't have to tell you not to be hard on yourself. I'll do that for you," said Bobby.

I pulled off my warm-ups and slapped my number on my left hip. "I got it, Bobby." My mind drifted back to the countless episodes of me sitting in the emergency room over the past two years.

The roar of the crowd brought me back to the moment. I looked deeply into Bobby's eyes. The eyes of the man who had never lost hope in me. And I knew that beyond all his insanity and over the top training sessions, he still held on to his belief in me.

He couldn't pass up being Bobby. "To be honest, if you break up that Russian threesome, I'll be content with that. But only this year. We'll take the gold in the Olympics."

"Got it, Bobby!" I said, this time with a little more emphasis on his name.

This stilled him for a moment, until he faded off and returned to take his seat in the stands.

I lined up in lane five, with Russians to my right and left in six and four. At the sound of the second whistle, my hips rose, and I anticipated the clapping of the gun.

# CHAPTER 25

"And I did what I set out to do, claiming the silver. No Russian sweep," I say.

"That's amazing," says the little boy from before.

The reporter from before interrupts. "How did you fare in ninety-two? The Olympics?"

"Really good. I ended up running both the hundred meter and the hundred hurdles, making the US team in both. As far as the Olympics are concerned, I won the hundred, but tripped the last hurdle, and tumbled across the finish line in fifth."

"Was it more due to a lack of focus from all the pressure of coming back to the sport?"

"Not at all. Actually, I was *very* focused. I didn't feel like I had to prove myself to anyone because I was doing this for me. I had made that contract with myself, Bobby was fully behind me, and my support system kept encouraging me to do my best. My only goal that year, beyond running and getting back to the big stage, was to go all out each and every race and let the chips fall where they may. I did that. I pulled down the American record that year from twelve sixty-one to twelve forty-eight. Just a little too fast in the case of the hurdles. I couldn't control my speed and simply ran out of room. "

"So imagine what you would've run if you didn't –"

"Hit that hurdle," I say, cutting him off. "Yeah, I know. But I don't think about it that way. People say the hurdles was a jinx, but in all truth, me not winning the hurdles in the Olympics is what kept me competing year after year. In ninety-three, I ended up grabbing gold medals for both the hundred sprint and the hurdles. It was the first time in forty-six years that that happened. Even broke the American record in the process, ironically dropping the time down to point *forty-six*.

"But one of my biggest honors ever that year was when Wilma Rudolph herself grabbed me by the arm and pulled me to the side at World Championships, and told me she had been watching me and that she recognized my accomplishments. She told me to keep up the good work. I was humbled. Here I was, with the woman who beat polio commending me on my success. Later on, I ended up presenting her with an ESPN award at 'The Great Ones' event. God has given me this platform which also allowed me to become a voice, not only for athletes, but for the families of Grave's disease itself."

# CHAPTER 26

"Hey, Gail. Come check this out!" Mike yelled from the couch.

*Oh boy, what does he have now? He's always rummaging through old tapes or finding some real interesting stuff on the internet,* I thought.

I scooted into the living room and plopped down on the couch next to him. The excitement in his voice was infectious, making my heart bound into my throat. "This is so crazy," I said in a whisper. Even the days of running track and field in front of thousands of fans, and being broadcast over the airways into millions of homes, couldn't prepare me for what was in front of me. We watched my appearance on The Robert Townsend Show and my previously recorded interview on the Oprah Winfrey Show. I had never gotten the chance to see them.

"So, tell me, Gail: how does it feel to be the face of a very new, rare disease?" asked Oprah.

The crowd erupted as she did her best to break the ice.

"It feels good, Oprah," I replied with a smile.

"But really, Gail, you have become voice for so many men and women all around the world who suffer with Grave's disease. And your story has brought thousands of dollars towards the research of the disease, along with some much needed awareness."

"Yes, it's weird because you never go through life expecting that some tragedy will be used to elevate others. But one day, I woke up, and there I was, becoming an inspiration for such a rare disease."

Oprah interrupts, "It's more than inspirational." She pans to the audience for a second and then back to me. "You know what everyone used to call you, The Undiagnosed Girl. Well, you are not that woman anymore. You are a world and Olympic champion, and you did it in spite of what doctors and naysayers thought in light of your plight. What's the first word that comes to your mind when you think of that?"

"Hope, Oprah. I know that God has a path and a purpose for me, and I am just so humbled to be used at this point to uplift others while bringing more and more visibility to this disease, so that others can be inspired and renew their hope."

Oprah nodded and looked away to the camera. "We'll be right back in a moment with more from Gail Devers."

The commercials rolled, and Mike took me by the hand and squeezed. "You look damn good on TV, baby."

"Odd how I seem so different with so many layers of clothing on, versus my running gear."

Mike stroked his chin. "Humph, is that what it was?"

"Whatever," I said.

"I feel like I should be doing something more for the people with Grave's disease. I went so long without being diagnosed. It almost ruined me. I know that there are more people out there living a life of pain."

"Like what?" he asked.

"I don't know, maybe a crusade to encourage people to be more proactive in getting assessed for Grave's Disease."

"You mean: like a campaign of some kind? Didn't you do something similar to that years ago with your Gland Central Campaign?  You could contact Penny from Fleishman Hillard and see about revamping it. "

My eyes widened. "That's why they pay you the big bucks... that brain of yours.  Awesome idea! We could reassemble the team, get phlebotomist on board, and set up remote testing centers to test stimulating hormones levels."

"I'm sure it couldn't be that hard to set up."

"Do you really think we could do it again?"

"You've been to the Olympics, traveled all over the world, been on The Robert Townsend Show and Oprah Winfrey. You're virtually a television star. You can do anything," Mike said.

I tossed a pillow at his face. "Shut up. I'm serious. Where do we start for something like that?"

Mike sat silent, deep in thought.

The anxiety was overwhelming. "Hello...well."

"Call Penny."

"Good start."

Mike began searching his pockets. "Where did I place her number?"

"Funny," I said.

Mike's eyes narrowed as the words bounced around in his head. No laughing; that was good. But what was he truly thinking? Most of the time, if Mike had an idea, it'd shoot from his hip faster than the quickest draw in the West. Never the type for being short of words, this puzzled me. The anticipation threatened to suffocate me.

The idea buzzed around in my head, threatening to explode. But I feared it would sound too corny. "You know, this will take some work. You in?"

Mike raised two fingers, "Scouts honor."

"Boy, please. Everybody knows you weren't *no* Scout." I shook my head.

"Can't blame a man for trying."

I narrowed my eyes at him. "For real Mike. Are you in?"

He started scratching his head.

I couldn't take it anymore, and this was decidedly not the time to play games; at least not in my case. "Are you in?" I repeated in a loud voice.

Mike answered, "Yes babe, I'm in," with a smile. "I'm in."

# CHAPTER 27

"That year, we made our way into countless cities, setting up sites for testing and handed out endless pamphlets and brochures in an effort to educate the entire country," I say.

"That's amazing. So you turned your struggle into something positive. Joy from pain," says another reporter from the side. "Tell me, Gail, going back to the fall in nineteen ninety-two, would you mind reliving the details of that moment?"

"Actually, I'd like to move forward with what happened after ninety-two. As you could imagine, the sting of hitting that last hurdle was still fresh on my mind as ninety-three drew closer. The word redemption blazed in my mind like a neon sign. Any hurdle race after my fall was looked at as another step towards reclamation, nothing more. That's why I was able to do so well at the World's Championships; I was focused."

The reporter stares at my hands and cracks a smile. "No more long, sensational nails huh?"

"No. That is behind me now. I grew them long back then as a sign that I was back; that I had taken control of my disease. When I was sick, my nails would break so easily. So when I finally had the ability to grow them out, I did so."

"With flair, might I add," he says.

"You may," I reply.

"So, with Grave's disease somewhat behind you after ninety-three, what was there left to do?" he asks.

"Run. My pursuit of that hurdle Olympic gold medal kept me going. I wasn't going to stop going after it just because of my previous loss. I knew that no one was faster than me in between the hurdles, and it was my speed that was my own downfall. I felt as if the only thing that could stand in my way was me. That is, unless you count another string of injuries. In ninety-four, I was sidelined by a pulled hamstring and a case of sciatica. By ninety-six, I was back on track, literally, chasing Olympic fame."

# CHAPTER 28

"The one thing Gail will have to do is focus on her lane, keeping her speed under control; that is her big problem," said Carol Lewis.

I crouched down and loaded into the blocks, analyzing the situation before me. There would only be one person to my left in lane one. The rest of the field would be to my right. That meant that all I'd have to do was focus on the pack in my right periphery.

"Get set," said the starter, raising his pistol.

My hips rose.

I held my breath.

Boom!

I exploded down the track.

The roar of the crowd became a distant memory in my head as the first hurdle approached. The runner to my left cleared the hurdle just a hair before me. To my surprise, it was not the pack, but *she* who gave me the biggest challenge.

*Concentrate, Gail*, I thought, as my legs began to pick up speed.

Mid-way through the race, I was out in front, with no one in my sights. All I had to do now was control my speed and clear the hurdles. I jumped the last one – albeit, a little higher than I'd have liked – and sprinted to the finish line, safe.

The tape paused.

"See right there, Gail," Bobby said, pointing at the screen with the remote. "You started to get a little high over those last three. You sacrificed technique for speed. You made it through to the finals, but that could cost you in the finals if you do it again."

"I got it, Bobby," I said.

"Don't give me that 'got it, Bobby, stuff.' I mean it. You can kill the field and the American Record if you just do it. After this, the Olympics again. Just relax, and try not to think about it."

I nodded, quiet this time, mindful not to respond. To do so would only let Bobby in my head—even more that he already was. I tried to block him out as much as possible during those times. With the finals coming up the next day, I had to find a way to not think about running, or falling, for that matter. When film review was over, I exited his room, and headed back to my own.

That night flew by like lightning, and before I knew it, I was back on the track, awaiting the announcement of the finalists as I stood in my lane, staring down lane four at the finish line; ten barriers in my sights. This time, unlike the last, I didn't remember who was in what lanes. My mind was only preoccupied with thoughts of me.

My lane.

My hurdles.

My race.

I tucked down in my blocks, loaded my back foot in, and placed my front knee down on the rubberized floor. My fingers pressed into the floor as I leaned forward. My body stilled, paralyzed, as I took my last breath and awaited the sound of the gun.

My hips rose.

Boom!

In a flash, the race was over, and I crossed the tape alone. One of the smoothest races I'd ever run. I applauded and took a slight bow, hugging the other competitors. I'd done it; won the US Championships. Soon, I'd be here again, on this same track. Atlanta, Georgia, site of the next Olympic Games.

## CHAPTER 29

"I ended up coming in fourth in the Olympic finals for the hurdles, but I won the hundred meters," I say. "But this time, I credited the other women for running some fantastic times. It was less of my technique and lack of focus, and more about their execution."

"Miss Gail," a small voice says from the front row.

I kneel down and meet the face of the voice. A young girl – sporting the cutest bright red and black warm-ups with matching shoes – stares back at me. "Yes?" I ask.

"What was your favorite race?" she asks.

"First, you have to tell me your name."

"My name is Ebony," she says.

I grip my chin firmly. "Hmm, Ebony, that's a good question. You know, with all this hurdle talk, you'd think it was the hurdles, huh?"

She nods.

"Well, actually, I have to say that I had an amazing time running the four by one hundred meter relay. I have three gold medals in that race. One for the Olympics, one for the World Championships, and the other in the Pan Am Games."

"That's cool," Ebony replies.

"Yep, it is cool. And it was fun, too. But my hundred meter sprinting days weren't too bad, either."

"I know. My mommy says that you were the only person to ever win back-to-back Olympic titles in the hundred, and win back-to-back hurdle titles at the World Championships," Ebony says.

"Wow, you did your homework, Ebony," I tease.

"Yep." Ebony holds up a pair of track spikes. "I'm going to be a World Champion one day in the hundred meters, too."

"Enough chatting. How about we do what we came here to do?"

Her big eyes blink and her mouth twitches as she ponders my question. "What's that?"

I poke her in the stomach. "Some training, silly."

"Yeah, that would be best."

"I agree."

"Miss Devers, is that all you do is train?" she asks.

# PART IV: FINISH LINE

# CHAPTER 30

"Most people, who make it in life, say that there is a time of transition in their life where things really come together. It could be a great loss of some kind, or a moment of breakthrough. Do you recall any such time in your life?" Doug asks.

"I remember in nineteen ninety-seven, Dad had gotten sick and just wanted to continue enjoying life and the Phillips were known for taking *road trips*. So I accompanied them on a trip to Vegas. At a little amusement park just outside of Vegas we rode bumper cars and what was known then as the fastest roller coaster in the world. It moved so fast we had to take off hats, jewelry...the whole nine. I mean, tie down anything moving. It was so much fun.

"Later that day, we had all gone to eat and Mike and I decided to take an evening stroll; take in the Vegas night scene. It was magical. Mike and I became oblivious to our surroundings, becoming entrenched in our own conversations – as we were known to do."

# CHAPTER 31

"Beautiful night, huh?" Mike asked.

"Yeah," I said, looking at the sky. "I wonder how many are up there?"

"What?"

"The stars. I mean, they say billions, but how do they know?"

Mike huffed. "Well, I'm less inclined to worry about those than the ones we can see right in front of us."

I turned to meet him. His face wore a smug smile. "Really?"

"What? That line too much for you?"

"Not really, just a little over the top."

"I don't think so at all. I know a lot more about you than you know, Gail. It's people like you that really get under my skin."

"What?" I gasped. Now he'd done it.

He fanned his palms at me. "Hear me out for a minute. People like you are studs. You're good at what you do. You barely have to exert yourself to beat people, and yet, you carry yourself with such grace and humility that you make it look easier than it is." He chuckled. "It's really annoying."

"Thank you, I think?"

"No, thank you. Being around people like you is inspiring. You are a star. One I can see, and one I can believe in. My family sees it, too."

"I'm just doing what I know to do with the gifts I have."

"You're doing a great job at it."

It was the first conversation I'd had with someone of the opposite sex, where they didn't make me feel as if I was a piece of meat or a trophy. It was nice, and I would remember it for a long time to come.

# CHAPTER 32

"Unfortunately, Dad passed later that year and this really brought Mike and I closer because I then found myself being a needed support to Mike and the family. They would travel like the *Griswold's* – including luggage falling out on the freeway – to my track meets and I would drive back with them. Mike would handle the night drives because Monica joked that Chris couldn't see at night. I'd be right there riding shotgun and Mike and I would talk the whole six hour trip back. Mom had commented how cute it was that we flapped our lips non-stop, especially since Mike is not known to be a talker. We grew closer, realizing we had so much in common and truly enjoyed one another's company. He always took it upon himself to carry the bulk of my emotional distresses and provided me with encouraging words. Even at my lowest, I knew I could depend on him. He did whatever he could to manage whatever was wearing away at me. So to sum it all up; it was a year of pain and gain. But I grew stronger because of it."

"Wow, amazing. That's so wonderful," says Doug. "Well, Miss Devers, I want to thank you again for coming by to share your story with us today on 1390 WPOK radio."

"Thank you, Doug. It's a pleasure to be here," I say.

"If you're just tuning in, we've been talking with World Champion, Olympic gold medalist, legend, and Sprint Diva, Gail Devers, about her life. The past trials, successes, and failures that shaped her into the woman she is today. You mentioned earlier, Gail, how persevering through the hard times helped you to develop your testimony, and more importantly, how some of your failures kept you motivated to get to the next level of where God wanted you to be. I find that very intriguing because I don't think the majority of our listeners, or people in general, have enough hindsight to see things that way. How did you develop this ideal? Which one came first: the failure, the success, or the perspective?"

"That's a good question, Doug. I think the hardest part about going through something is that you have to *go through it* first, then, as you survive whatever you've been subjected to, you have the chance to think back in retrospect and analyze the situation more clearly. Looking back at my situation and circumstances, I can definitely say that there were times when I wanted to give up and just do me. But I kept hearing this voice in my head that told me to push on, finish the journey, and just wait. So I leaned more and more on family and friends to help me endure and develop the patience for the process."

Doug nods. "That's amazing. So, it is important for people to develop a support group, or to at least have a group of people to lean on, in trying times?"

"Absolutely. I don't know how I would have made it this far without them. I think my own stubbornness carried me about halfway through, but those supporters gave me the push to stay the course."

Doug gestures to me with his hands in a stop sign motion. "Once again, listeners, we're honored to have Gail Devers here on the radio show, talking about her life story. If you are interested in speaking with Gail, we will be opening up the lines very shortly. When we do, just call the number and hold on the line." He pauses, looks over at the producer, and motions as though he is breaking a stick with his hands. "We're going to go to a quick commercial break and return soon. You're listening to the real talk here on 1390 WPOK radio, the *Douggie Dee Show*."

Doug removes his headphones, and leans in to me. "When we come back, I'm going to ask a couple more questions, and then open the phone lines for callers to get in a few."

"Okie dokie," I say.

After a few minutes, Doug comes alive again. "That's right, listeners, you are currently tuned in to the hardest working man on radio, *Douggie Dee*, and my guest today, is the ultra-talented, very successful, Gail Devers."

"Hi, Doug," I say into the mic.

"Now, Gail, I've got to ask you this question. You've done just about everything on the track. World Champion, record holder, collegiate champion. So, now, what is there left for Gail to do?"

"Well, Doug, I'm proud to say that I am a very happy mother of two, and my husband Mike and I are thrilled to be parents. I know now that everything I went through was to prepare me to raise my little ones to be strong, independent women. There was a moment when one of my girls fell really sick. I mean, *really* sick, and it landed her in the hospital. I remember standing over her in the hospital bed, and she asked me if I would take her place. I simply told her 'no,' because it was her plight to

143

deal with. If I lived her life for her and took everything away from her, then how would she ever learn how to survive? It may sound harsh to the average person, but my faith allows me to trust a higher power."

Doug's eyes widened. "Man, I see how you made it through everything." He smiles sarcastically. "I read an article about you once where you said you left your coach because you wanted to stay motivated. Well, let's flashback for a moment. Take us back to that time."

"Now, that is a testimony in and of itself. It was after the nineteen ninety-seven, ninety-eight season. I had gone through yet another injury where I was sidelined by an Achilles' wound. I had to stay in a fill ankle and lower leg Multi Podus boot for months on end. The following year, I was back on the track, regaining my ninety-nine World title in the hurdles. That led me to the two-thousand Olympic trials, where I set the American Record of twelve thirty-three. But, in Sydney, during the games, I got injured again and had to discontinue competition."

# CHAPTER 33

"Hey, Bobby," I said, stepping into his office. It was the coldest the room had ever been before. He looked up at me from the desk with an equally frigid stare.

"Gail," he grunted, looking back down at a form he was busy filling out on his desk.

"Can I talk with you for a moment?"

Bobby lifted his glasses from his eyes and matched my gaze. "Sure, what's up?"

I closed the distance between us and sat in the chair in front of him. "Since Sydney, well, I've been giving it a lot of thought and I don't want to drag this out. I can only say it the best way I know how. I –"

"Want to seek other arrangements, right?"

My mouth dropped. "What?"

Bobby reclined in his chair. "You want to go out on your own."

"But how did –"

"Come on, Gail. I've sat in this seat many times before. Athletes come and go out that door, year after year. I know a last victory lap when I see it." He sighed heavily. "So, all that's left is for you to tell me why."

"Well, I just think I'm, well...getting older, and you have a huge stable of athletes now. I'm getting injured every other year, and you don't need to waste your time baby-sitting me. That's all. Besides, I want to see if I can do it on my own."

"On you own? What is this, some mid-life crisis, Devers?"

"I need to find something else other than winning to keep me motivated. I prayed and prayed on this for the longest time. The events in Sydney kind of forced my decision."

Bobby held the tip of his glasses in the corner of his mouth. "And you think that's best to be done on your own?"

"I won't be alone, Bobby. I'll have God with me. Have you ever heard of that poem *Footprints In The Sand*?"

"This ain't no Hallmark greeting card, Devers. This is the real world. There are women everywhere who want to take you down, just to make a name for themselves. I know I've been busy lately with this new slew of athletes, but you know you always hold a special position with me. You're more than just another number."

The tears filling my eyes threatened to overrun, but I did my best to restrain them as I attempted to speak. "I must do this, Bobby. I'm grateful for everything you've given and done for me. But I know the time is right."

Bobby took his glasses off and laid them on the desk. He stood and came around to the other side to meet me face to face.

I stood.

"Well, I don't like it one bit. One: because I'm going to truly miss you. And two: because now, I have to coach against your butt. But I respect your decision."

We embraced, and I held on to him just long enough for me to quell my tears. I pulled back and froze for a moment. This was it; the end to a chapter of my life that I never really made peace with. I walked towards the door and grabbed the knob, just as Bobby called out to me.

"Hey, Devers," he said.

"Yeah, Bobby," I replied.

He pointed a taunting finger at me and said, "Don't choke."

I smiled. "I never do."

# CHAPTER 34

"That year, I trained like a beast, waking up at crazy hours in the morning, forcing myself to stay one step ahead of the competition. I was convinced that Bobby and the rest of the world would be doing their best to gun after me," I say.

"What was it like without Bobby?" asks Doug.

"It was weird at first. I mean, Bobby had been with me during all my toughest competitions in college and as a pro. It wouldn't be enough for me to just go out there and compete. I needed an edge. So, for the first time in my career, I attempted to run the hurdles indoors. My goal – the American record."

"How'd that work out for you?" jokes Doug.

"Pretty good, actually. Set the American record twice in the same season. I even started calling my support team the Heaven Bound Track Club. A group of athletes that trained together with Christ on their mind and in their hearts."

"That's profound," Doug chimes.

"Indeed. The season was going a lot better than even I predicted it would; at least, from a hurdling perspective. I really didn't have any time to sprint train because I was busy focusing on being so technical with the hurdles. But I figured the short hurdle work was doing a good enough job of keeping me quick, and I would be good for the start of the outdoor season. That's what I hoped, anyway. So, I decided to jump in the open one hundred meters at the *Prefontaine Classic* in Oregon."

"And let me guess: you set another record?" Doug interrupts.

"No, but I did run close to a personal best."

Doug shakes his head. "Gail, why don't we take a call from the listener world, and give you a chance to address your fans."

"Sounds good to me, Doug."

"Caller, you're on. Please tell us your name and where you're from," announces Doug.

A voice careens from the over the line. "Hey, Gail."

"Hello," I return.

"My name is Chandra Steel, and I'm one of your biggest fans, and I ran for a short time in college, but could never break under eleven seconds in the hundred. How did you go about keeping your focus when you set your mind to setting goals and personal bests?" she asks.

"Good question, Chandra. Well, I think the hardest thing about competing is really about doing that one thing that makes you finally believe that you can compete at a high level and win. Once you've done that, once you've finally broken through and have gotten on that list of elites, you never settle for being in the back of the pack again. For me, as I was coming back and doing it all on my own, it wasn't until the two-thousand one season, after I endured another injury, that I found my own stride again."

I talked to Mike about injuries, training and just life in general. As always he was there to encourage me. I know you can do it, he said and you know I'll be here for you. It may not always be easy, but I know you.

"There you go with that again," I said.

"No, I'm serious. I do know you and you thrive off challenges, look at your life and what you've overcome."

"And you want me to tell you what I really know—Yeah, why don't you enlighten me," I said.

"Okay, I know over the years we've gotten close, we've become best friends. I know I plan to always be here to carry the bulk of your emotional distress. I know at my lowest I could depend on you and you depend on me. I know that we are good for each other and together. And I know I'm going to marry you someday."

This made my heart skip, but why? I had known Mike for 17 years and had never thought of getting involved with much less dating my friend's brother and never did I think he would want to be with me like that. Surely he was joking.

"Whatever mike."

"No I'm serious."

I dangerously narrowed my eyes at him. "I hope you're not trying to marry me out of sympathy," I joked.

"Never that. I just think that you deserve a good man; someone who knows you and understands what you're going through and is willing to help see you through it all. I told you a long time ago that you were a star, and I stand by it." He paused to stare at his fingers, fidgeting. It was the first time I'd ever seen him in a disposition even remotely close to being nervous. He looked back up at me. "What if I asked you out one day for dinner? What would you say?"

"I'd say: it depends."

Mike leaned back. "Depends on what?"

"Where are you going to take me?"

"Shoot. McDonalds, of course. Only the best."

"Well, in that case, I'd say yes."

We shared a meal and smile that day, and never looked back. I think that was the first time I really looked at Mike. *He's cute,* I thought to myself, but I couldn't have him getting the *big head* so I kept it to myself. But the irony is that we discussed how we both had been married previously, divorced, built a friendship, and become business associates, so the thought of ever being married was like *ugh.* Actually neither of us had any plans of ever marrying again. Been there, done that, not going back. But God had other plans. We eloped that next year, in a small ceremony in Vegas one weekend, without telling anyone, and have been conquering together ever since.

# CHAPTER 35

"All right, Gail. All you have to do is win this final race, and you'll be deemed the Golden League Champion. They give cars away Gail. I even think they give gold bars," said Mike emphatically.

"They do not," I said, laying on my back with my feet up, taking a moment to rest my feet before the final.

Mike knelt down beside me. "Seriously, no joking."

I shook my head dismissively, silent. I had already dosed off into the zone, getting ready for the race just minutes away.

Moments later, I stood at the starting line and stared down the track at the ten barriers before me, awaiting the clap of the starting pistol. A win here would definitely set me back in pace to be the world's fastest female, and I didn't have any plans of missing out on that opportunity.

The starting official raised one hand overhead. "On your mark," he said.

I squatted down and loaded myself backwards into the blocks.

"Get set," he said.

My hips rose. The tension in my feet resonated through my legs and up into my fingertips.

*Concentrate, Gail*, I thought.

Boom!

My foot skipped out of the back block and landed out in front of me just as my front one lifted underneath my hips. It was the best start of the summer season. There was no way I was going to lose.

I walked over the hurdles like I was playing hopscotch. In no time flat, I was crossing the finish line.

I'd done it. I made a name for myself again, and I was ready to take my place on the A-list of track and field again.

Mike met me at the bottom of the stairs leading into the locker-room, holding what appeared to be a gold bar. "Is that what I think it is?" I asked.

His eyes skipped to the gold bar in his hand. He holds it up teasing, "Lula lula lula, this is mine," he said.

"Fine by me. I don't like chocolate anyway."

He unwrapped it and took a huge bite. "I know."

Mike leaned in and gave me a strong hug. The warmth of his skin cooled the adrenaline coursing through my veins. "Thank you," I whispered.

"Now, it's time to get out of here." He released me. "Come on, I'm hungry."

# CHAPTER 36

"I used that race to set the tone for the next three years, for which I was able to remain uninjured. I set the indoor record again for the sixty meter hurdles in two thousand two, and then won the indoor and outdoor two-thousand three World Championships in the hurdles," I say.

"Again," Chandra says over the speakers, "how did you get in that mindset that you would rebound, especially after all the changes?"

"Through lots of prayer, Chandra. God assured me I was going to be okay and I was." I rest my index finger along my temple. "I think I set the record for being ranked number one in the world in the hurdles for one hundred and twenty-four consecutive months back then. I was also noted to have the most races in a single season, in which I ran under twelve and a half seconds in the hurdles. I concluded my self-training run with a sprint gold medal in Budapest at the Indoor World Championships in two thousand four.

"Unbelievable, Gail," says Doug. "Take us back a little bit to your high school days when you just started running. What was that like?"

"I remember the first time my mom was able to get off work to see me run was at Metro League finals in High School, and I was running the three hundred meter low hurdles. Angel Dresser and I called ourselves the one-two hurdle crew. The gun sounded and we took off. I tripped and fell over the second hurdle, and Angel – being a true friend and not competitor – turned around and came back to help me. I remember her yelling, 'We have to do it together!' despite the fact that I was yelling back at her, 'Go! Run!'" I chuckle as my mind flashes back to the scene. "I guess will and heart took over, so I got up, finished the race, and somehow won. Someone had taped the meet, and when I fell you could hear the crowd saying, 'Get up, Gail! Come on, you can do it.' My mother's voice rose above the crowd, crying out, 'Stay down, baby! I'm coming!'"

Doug bursts into laughter. "You've got to be kidding me! Wow."

"Nope, a true mother's statement. She was nothing like I am with my kids. When they fall, I tell them: you're good, get up."

"No guts, no glory," adds Doug.

"*Exxxaaactly*. We once had a track meet at Southwest College, and it got so late that it was pitch black. The meet director wanted to cancel the meet, but everyone complained, and the parents went to get their cars and pull them up close to the track. One by one, they shined headlights on the track so that we could finish. I always say most things stem from your childhood. You don't quit; you find a way to get it done."

"We have a tweet from Twitter that came in from @JollieHunter. She asks, "What's one of the funniest times you ever had while competing?"

"That's a hard one." I rub my lip, thinking. "Oh, yeah," I snap. "At the nineteen ninety-two Olympics, Coach Bobby and our trainer could not ride on the athletes' bus to go practice, so they followed in a car behind the bus. We got to a turnabout, and the cops detained Bobby. Locals jumped out of cars, everybody had arms flailing, and we watched from the bus until we couldn't see anymore; then we turned around and kept it moving. When we got to the track, we warmed up like nothing was wrong. Everybody kept looking at Jackie and me like we had two heads or something.

"One lady finally asked, 'Aren't you guys concerned about not having your coach?' Our response? 'He's not running for us.' Our mindset was: we came to win. Bobby had done his part, and we were ready to go do ours. When we were almost done, Bobby showed up and everyone told him we didn't care. If they took him to jail, we hoped that they would have let him watch the race on TV. He just laughed and said, 'That's cold, but true.'"

Doug scrolls through his phone. "Let me find another one," he says. "@Angle tweeted this question, Gail. 'How much did you put into preparing for competition?'"

"At major championships and the Olympic games," I start, "people with credentials need a place where taxis can drop them off close to the track. If you decide not to stay in the Village in order to concentrate, you are left to get to the track on your own, and may be walking among fans and have to allow extra time in case you are stopped for 'auto grams,' as they say in Europe. I was a timely person; I timed out how long for my warm-up based on the time I had to report to the call room, and put on everything—from being stopped to sign autographs, to taking bathroom breaks.

"Also, fans don't realize how far athletes sometimes have to walk just to get from the warm-up to the call room. Sometimes up and down stairs, over bridges, down corridors. Might be another fifteen minutes, so you have to adjust your warm-up time. They usually give a walk-through a few days before the meet starts, and you may wonder, 'What for? I'm just running hundred meters straight down the track.' But really, it adds to your mental fortitude to know the track and visualize yourself competing."

"Speaking of competition," says Doug. "A lot has been made about the authenticity of competition nowadays with player bans in track and field, and steroid use in baseball and football. What is your viewpoint on these topics? Are the bans tough enough, or do we need stricter policies?"

"I'm glad you brought that up, Doug. Drug testing was a big part of my career. In and out of competition, random knocks on the door at all hours and anywhere. You have to give account of your whereabouts, so if your name comes up they can find you. I've been tested coming off airplanes at airports, movies, friends and family's homes. Real funny! Some may regard it as a bother. I look at it like this: if I have to use the restroom and you want my pee, have at it. I've nothing to hide. In our sport, we have rules and regulations that govern our sport to keep it on the up and up. If you don't like the rules, and can't or don't want to play by them, get out of the sport. Sports are a privilege, not a right!

"The one thing I will say is: we, as athletes, have to take more responsibility for ourselves. We must know and abide by the rules at all times. There are systems in place for just about everything. We have to be advocates for ourselves in order to safeguard ourselves, and our sport, from negativity. We are to list and have a paper trail of any and all supplements taken. Anything entering your body is your responsibility. If you are sick, there is a hotline number to call and ask if you can take certain medications. If it is prohibited, they will give you an alternative that is legal. That phone call is recorded and documented. When I went to the dentist, I had my dentist fax the name of the Novocain so there was a record. I left nothing to chance. I didn't take anyone at face value. Didn't drink from open containers or let anyone give me anything. When it comes down to it, you have to take care of you because it will be your name they drag through the mud.  At drug testing, you are to list everything you have taken, not come back and declare after the fact.

"If stiffer punishments are enforced, we would discourage wrongdoing, make athletes responsible for themselves, clean up our sport, change the public perception, set examples for generations to follow, and ensure that there is a sport that follows the Olympic Oath of fair play.  The oath says: In the name of all the competitors, I promise that we shall take part in this Olympic Games and respecting abiding by the rules which govern them, committing ourselves to a sport without doping and without drugs, in the true spirit of sportsmanship, for the glory of sport and the honor of our teams. I take this oath truthfully in sports and in life.

"Now, our rule says Zero Tolerance in the case of a positive test. I believe Zero Tolerance should mean just that. For me, that means lifetime ban for all found guilty regardless if it is a coach, manager, trainer, mom, dad, whomever. It doesn't matter. And everything should be erased from records books. Like I said before: competing in sports is a privilege. I will say this though, our laws state that if person is found guilty and serves their determined ban, whether suspension or punishment, they can come back and are allowed to compete again. This participation should be without continuous negative commentary from fans, press, fellow athletes, or otherwise. The constant dwelling on negativity does nothing for the sport but breed more negativity. We as a sport cannot continue to nourish the black cloud that looms over it. If we do, 'grey skies will never clear up.' Change comes from action, not talking. Be about it, don't just talk about it. We need to lobby for changes in the system, and uphold the Zero Tolerance stance to its fullest. Zero Tolerance should not be with conditions. It should be laid out with no bargaining."

Doug nods slowly. "Sounds like you are very passionate about this, Gail?"

"I am. I just think, that as an athlete, if you know the consequences are so severe, you will try harder not be easily persuaded or leave yourself open to be taken advantage of. You will take the necessary precautions and not take chances with your career and reputation."

"How about family life? When did you know you'd marry Mike?" asks Doug.

"There is a song by Boyz II Men called: *I Finally Know*, talking about the person you've been searching for to love, and that person is only around when you're around. That was my *ah-ha* moment, and from that point forward, my heart and soul opened up. No longer was I wondering or searching for love. I married my best friend, Mike, who had been there all the time, and peace rests in my heart forever. After becoming a wife, I still had work to do, so there wasn't time for kids. I did know that my age could be a factor, but still, there was trust that when it was time, it would work out."

"We have a lot of female listeners who tune in to the show," says Doug. "You're now a career woman, but were a professional athlete. I'm sure many of them are wondering how you made it all work. How did family play into your career?"

"It wasn't easy. After the two thousand four Olympics, when I got injured for the umpteenth time, I refused to be carried off the track. Somehow, Mike made it onto the track, and I allowed him to assist me while I limped off it.

"I remember having some quiet time in the shower to contemplate what to do next. That night, I remember knowing the time was right, and Mike and I decided to have a child. Now, with this, came a whole new chapter in my life. I was so excited for this new adventure. We got pregnant right away, and I was looking forward to all the stories I had heard about. When I ran, my meal of choice in Europe was spaghetti either with just noodles or with sauce, so when I was pregnant, I looked forward to craving crazy stuff. I ate exactly the same spaghetti! Boring! And all my friends hated me, because I had no morning, noon or night sickness...no cravings...nothing. I went out and bought cute maternity clothes and no-one even noticed I was pregnant. From the back, you couldn't even tell. I was seven-and-a-half to eight months along before my neighbor even noticed and asked, 'Are you having a baby?' I mumbled under my breath, 'Well, it's about time someone noticed. I've only been walking around, sticking my stomach out for months.'

"Life was great. I gained seventeen pounds, and delivered a baby girl, and named her Karsen. We had to have a C-section. Again, best-laid plans don't always work out. I was hoping to deliver naturally, but God's way is the best way. After having Karsen, I started training again, just to get back in shape, but my focus had changed. It was about motherhood and I loved it. My warm-up consisted of me pushing the jogger stroller around the track, and then Mike would place the jogger as a cone where I was to stop, and he would hold Karsen and film. Great man! Boy, life certainly does change after kids. Having so much fun, we added another baby to the mix: Miss Legacy. The girls would lie on my stomach, or across my legs, while I did sit ups, and they'd imitate me doing lunges or whatever.

"We were training athletes, football players, and college kids getting ready for the combine, being parents and traveling. Life was good! The football aspect of this was a new venture, but exciting. I appreciated and loved that they realized they had one shot and needed to maximize full potential. Practices were awesome and intense. I would tell them to go through the speed ladder, and when they were done, I would just stand there, with arms folded. When they caught their breath, I'd yell 'Move it! It's called speed ladder for a reason. If I wanted you to tip-toe, I would have put down some tulips. This is how it's done.' Oh, the looks on their faces. But that's when practice got fun! Most of them made it their duty to outdo me. For one: because I was the coach. And two: because I'm a girl. It was too funny! We traveled to their pro-days for support, and most of them are still playing or involved in the sport in some capacity today.

"The girls went everywhere with us. I believe life itself is a learning experience. They have more travel miles than most. It was funny because, in the beginning, I use to say they just think I'm the funny lady that makes them smile: Mommy! Nothing more, nothing less. But as we would go places, I remember Karsen was two, asking me 'Why do people call you Gail Dee-Vers, and why do you keep writing it on paper for them?' I told her, 'People just like the way I write my name Gail Devers.' She then started standing at the top of the stairs at home calling, 'Mommy! Mommy!' If I didn't answer right away, she'd say, 'Gail Dee-Vers, I'm talking to you!' She was way too grown and observant back then. I take that back. She still is. I guess she figured Gail Dee-Vers would listen; Mommy, not so much."

We both share a laugh. "That's great," Doug says amongst the laughter.

"I wouldn't trade the world for my family," I say.

Doug straightens. "Who would? Well, it has been a pleasure hosting you here today on the *Douggie Dee Show*. Can you just summarize your career: the ups and the downs, and the trials which have literally made you who you are today?"

"Sure, Doug. All or nothing. That's how I live my life. One speed. Your destiny is wrapped up in your belief. It's what I call the 'just make it and take it' philosophy. No one will give it to you; you have to be willing to earn it. I did my time, paid my dues on the rehab floor, and took my opportunities, and made best of them when my number came up. I preach this to my kids every day; success doesn't mean you need to have it all and win it all. It's about doing your best, and being satisfied with the outcomes: if, at the end, you know you gave it your all. And through it all, I've learned to depend on Jesus."

As Doug closes out the show, I lay down my headset and empty out from the recording booth. The cool air outside the radio station meets me as I head towards my car. A girl rides by on her bicycle and stares at me. I flash her a smile. She stops, turns around, and comes back to me.

"Are you Gail Devers, the legendary sprinter?" she asks.

"No," I say. "I'm Gail Devers, the messenger!"

# EPILOGUE

## Who is Gail Devers today?

I ran my last competitive race in two thousand seven: Millrose Games at age forty-plus and won, running a world leading time. As I said in my interview with Lewis Johnson, Jay-Z got it wrong: forty is the new twenty. Later that year, at seven months pregnant with Legacy in the belly, I commentated for Fox during the Peachtree road race in Atlanta, and ran the race with microphone and battery pack attached. Unfortunately, Mike felt he had to run with me because he didn't trust me to not maintain my heart rate at a safe level. I was proud of this accomplishment, and had fun interviewing competitors along the route. But I have to admit that when I got to one hundred fifty meters out from the finish line, I took off like I was in the Olympic Games (just had to do it).

Interestingly, I cannot really remember or imagine life without my family. Looking back, for me, I did not fully start living until I had kids. It feels like this was what I was meant to do. They give my life purpose and direction, and my new goal every day is to give guidance, be a positive role model, and give love. They are growing so fast and changing daily. They have their own unique personalities.

With the Internet, they have been able to look back and see my races, and see what I used to do before becoming cook, cleaning lady, playmate, and PTA mom. People ask if they are going to be runners, and Legacy replies, "I'm already faster than my mommy, so I don't have to run." Now, mind you, we have since addressed this comment. I *did* take her to the track and show her little tail the real deal.

Karsen has about seventeen things on her plate at once and still wants more. I try my best to steer them both down their own path, but I have to admit that they do appear to have the natural gift. I am proud and feel blessed that God picked me to be their mommy. They speak their minds, love everyone, and have their own relationship with God. They understand the house motto: "Be truthful at all times, and always do your best in everything you do."

These days, I work a lot with mentoring programs wanting to instill a sense of pride and confidence in our youth. I believe we all have inside of us what it takes to be successful. We have to believe it, find it, bring it out, and let it work. Sometimes, because of life's circumstances, influences, choices, environment, self-esteem — or lack thereof –and confidence in our abilities may waver. I believe it's the job of everyone to help uplift one another in order to change this world for the better.

In my career, I always tried to give time to the fans. You never know what a kind word will do to inspire others to dream big. In life today, I am the same. I've walked out of my spikes and into cute shoes, but the goal and journey walk is still the same. "To touch lives, and make a difference."

I volunteer at my kids' school most every day, helping teachers. I'm involved with athletics, music, science, and math groups, willing to do anything to assist our future generation. Recently, I've been busy "branding" myself, and have my hands in several things from active wear apparel, alternative beverages, how-to DVDs, e-books, books and journals, along with creating original Reality-TV programming. I am excited to be an Ambassador for IAAF (International Amateur Athletic Federation) and to work worldwide with national governing bodies that share the same mission. I'm so thankful for the opportunity to promote fitness, and globally change the world by spreading the message of human kindness through sports and inspire the universe. I love being able to give back to the sport that gave so much to me.

For me, life is about having goals and working to achieve them. I take life "one hurdle at a time," while looking towards the next hurdle. I have always recognized that life comes with many challenges and obstacles. We can choose to conquer or be conquered. I always choose to conquer.

Looking back over my career, I have no regrets; I'd do all the same again. I have learned valuable life lessons that have built character, personality, and stamina. I have found strength I didn't realize I already had. Without my experiences, I would not have had the opportunity to discover what was lying beneath the surface all along. Now, I will admit, sometimes I had to do some deep digging to bring that little box of strength up, depending on the circumstance I was faced with, but willing nonetheless to be a digger for Christ. My life is a battle for God, not me, to show God's goodness.

Now, I enjoy life, family, and love in their entirety every day, whether I'm skating with the kids, doing crafts, baking, speaking, or reading a book. I take nothing for granted, for all things have a purpose. I signed up in God's army a long time ago, and I'm not tired yet. I'm thankful to USATF and USOC and NCAA for bestowing the highest honor on me and inducting me into their Halls of Fame. Words cannot adequately describe the joy. For me, I just go about setting individual goals, not really addressing or viewing accomplishments, just being in the moment and working. It was not until I received acknowledgement of these honors, that I fully realized my blessings, which I hold very dear to my heart.

# FINAL WORDS FROM GAIL

In life, we make plans for how we want our lives to be, and quickly learn that the best-laid plans don't always work out the way we want them to. I've come to learn that with God in charge, it always works out the way it's supposed to be.

My original plans were to marry, go to the Olympics, become a teacher, have kids, and live out my life. As you read, that plan got twisted along the way, but in keeping with my visions, everything panned out just the way it needed to. However, it started with a whole group of people: coaches, friends, and family with different ideas, visions, wants, and desires. In the end, I am left with my abilities, faith, and belief in myself that takes me to new horizons, summits, valleys, and places unknown and unimaginable.

I cannot stress the importance of support systems. We all need it—that certain someone or group of people who has your back, no matter what. They may not say or do anything, but their presence speaks volumes. When I stepped out on my own, I called on my friends to rally around to help. Most were not involved in fitness. If I had to go on a road run, Sharyl would gather her kids and follow in her car for safety. James and Brian would go to the weight room with me, or time me. And Debra, Carlean, and Debbie would come and walk on the track while I worked out. Sonya would keep her pool open after hours, and bump up the heat so I could get in a pool work out. I don't do cold water!

I bought a Pomeranian and named him Kaleb—"faithful"—to be my workout partner. Unconventional, but it got the job done. If I had to run a 300, Kaleb would start, and cheat by cutting across the field so he was on the other side in front of me, and led the way, barking at me. I was determined not to let this tiny dog beat me, either.

I'm a warrior! I always come prepared for battle! I feel as if I have mounted up in God's army, and am thankful for the opportunity to show off His goodness. My purpose is to utilize my God-given ability to the fullest, and give God the glory. I have always asked for God's favor and blessing.

I look at a coach and a teacher as motivators, and in life, we all play these roles eventually. Our job is to motivate and inspire others to want to do their best, and hone their talents, and find their inner box that holds our strength, guts, will, heart, desire, passion, and *umph*!

My life is complete, and now it's time to put it into words, and hopefully inspire others to know that life is what YOU make it. It is important to find your own inner drive, which is innately in you, versus what someone may tell you. There is a burning flame within me, and a driving force that no coach or person can give me.

It started with a thought, then a challenge from my brother, then a dream that became the daily vision that I walk in, to find the necessary support needed to facilitate the direction that became my destiny, with the good, bad and the ugly. I share my personal mottos because I am trying to inspire a new generation to truly believe in *self*!

Never give up! We may not know why we are on this journey, but along the way, we learn we are stronger than we had thought. We learn about ourselves. We are strong, and have to have faith to believe each day that we gain strength and power to conquer all things, even when others deem it to be impossible.

Believe the unbelievable!

Work harder and smarter than you think others are working,

And never accept defeat!

We are regarded as being only as good as our last race or deed, because that's what People remember, so make it count!

In my life, I've had ups and downs, trials and tribulations but "Through it All"

Two verses from gospel singer Andre Crouch's song sum of my life thus far;

Through it All

I've been to lots of places

I've seen millions of faces

There's been times I felt so all alone;

But in my lonely hours

Jesus lets me know that I was his own

I thank God for the mountains,

And I thank Him for the valleys,

I thank Him for the storms he brought me through

For if I'd never had a problem,

I wouldn't know God could solve them,

I'd never know what faith in God could do

Through it all, through it all

I've learned to trust in Jesus,

I've learned to trust in God

Through it all, though it all

I've learned to depend upon His Word

# ABOUT GAIL DEVERS

Gail Devers is a retired three-time Olympic champion in track and field for the US Olympic Team. A young talent in the 100 m and 100 m hurdles, Devers was in training for the 1988 Summer Olympics, started experiencing health problems, suffering (among others) migraine and vision loss. She qualified for the Olympics 100 m hurdles, in which she was eliminated in the semi-finals, but her health continued to deteriorate even further.

In 1990, she was diagnosed with Graves' disease, and underwent radioactive iodine treatment, followed by thyroid hormone replacement therapy. During her radiation treatment, Devers began to develop blistering and swelling of her feet. Eventually, the sprinter could barely walk and had to crawl and/or be carried. A doctor considered amputating her feet.

Amazingly, Devers recovered after the radiation treatment was discontinued, and she resumed training. At the 1991 World Championships, she won a silver medal in the 100 m hurdles. Devers went on to win both World Championship and Olympic gold again and again.

**Follow Gail:**
**Twitter:**
@ImGailDevers
**Facebook:**
www.facebook.com/ImGailDevers

# ABOUT BRAXTON A. COSBY

Dr. Braxton A. Cosby, CEO of Cosby Media Productions, is a dreamer who plays around with ideas in his mind that he desires to bring to life in print and share with the entire world. Braxton is an eternal student who ventures to learn more and more each day and embraces the idea of facing challenges head on, accomplishing what people determine as impossible. Braxton is an award-winning author who has penned two Young Adult series: The School of Ministry and The Star-Crossed Saga. As you may have guessed, Braxton is related to world famous comedian Bill Cosby, who has passed on his talent of storytelling to his nephew to create tales that inspire and entertain. Braxton has his doctorate in Physical Therapy and is a certified personal trainer and sports nutritionist. Braxton's health book **FAT FREE FOR LIFE** has recently been released from Charisma House. Braxton is married with four lovely children and lives in Georgia.

**Follow Braxton:**

www.braxtoncosby.com

www.cosbymediaproductions.com

**Twitter:**

@BraxtonACosby

**Facebook:**

www.facebook.com/DrBraxtonCosby

Cosby Media Productions™

Entertaining the Mind, and Inspiring the Soul

www.cosbymediaproductions.com

Made in the USA
Middletown, DE
24 January 2020

83576769R00110